ALCOHOL PROBLEMS

TEXTBOOK
SERVICE

An insp   International Library
will glad   sideration for
course a   of 60 days
from rece   pted or
recommended for   use and   n a sale
of 12 or more copies the inspection copy may be retained   mpliments.
The Publishers will be pleased to receive suggestions for revised editions and new
titles to be published in this important international Library.

Pergamon Titles of Related Interest

Miller BEHAVIORAL TREATMENT OF ALCOHOLISM
Miller THE ADDICTIVE BEHAVIORS
Tittmar ADVANCED CONCEPTS IN ALCOHOLISM

Related Journals*

ADDICTIVE BEHAVIORS
ALCOHOL AND ALCOHOLISM
ALCOHOL AND DRUG RESEARCH
JOURNAL OF SUBTANCE ABUSE TREATMENT

*Free sample copy available upon request.

ALCOHOL PROBLEMS

Diagnosis and Treatment

David H. Knott, M.D., Ph.D.
Memphis Mental Health Institute

PERGAMON PRESS
New York • Oxford • Toronto • Sydney • Frankfurt

Pergamon Press Offices:

U.S.A.	Pergamon Press Inc., Maxwell House, Fairview Park, Elmsford, New York 10523, U.S.A.
U.K.	Pergamon Press Ltd., Headington Hill Hall, Oxford OX3 0BW, England
CANADA	Pergamon Press Canada Ltd., Suite 104, 150 Consumers Road, Willowdale, Ontario M2J 1P9, Canada
AUSTRALIA	Pergamon Press (Aust.) Pty. Ltd., P.O. Box 544, Potts Point, NSW 2011, Australia
FEDERAL REPUBLIC OF GERMANY	Pergamon Press GmbH, Hammerweg 6, D-6242 Kronberg-Taunus, Federal Republic of Germany
BRAZIL	Pergamon Editora Ltda., Rua Eça de Queiros, 346, CEP 04011, São Paulo, Brazil
JAPAN	Pergamon Press Ltd., 8th Floor, Matsuoka Central Building, 1-7-1 Nishishinjuku, Shinjuku, Tokyo 160, Japan
PEOPLE'S REPUBLIC OF CHINA	Pergamon Press, Qianmen Hotel, Beijing, People's Republic of China

Copyright © 1986 Pergamon Press Inc.

First printing 1986

Library of Congress Cataloging in Publication Data

Knott, David H.
    Alcohol problems.

    1. Alcoholism. I. Title. [DNLM: 1. Alcoholism--
diagnosis. 2. Alcoholism--therapy. WM 274 K72a]
RC565.K57   1986   616.86'1   85-21616
ISBN 0-08-032393-6
ISBN 0-08-032392-8 (pbk.)

Printed in Great Britain by A. Wheaton & Co. Ltd., Exeter

To my mother and father
To my wife Tara
To my sons, Kevin and Kepler

CONTENTS

ACKNOWLEDGMENTS

"He who is sick should find in the eyes of the physician a reflection of his own anguish and some recognition of the uniqueness of his suffering."

Illich — *Medical Nemesis*

To: W.D., W.P., J.B., M.H., C.A., J.S., and the thousands of persons who suffer from the disease alcoholism who have been and continue to be my teachers.

I am particularly indebted to the following individuals:

Richard R. Overman, PhD, who, as my scientific father and major professor, guided me through the early years of training; James D. Beard, PhD, whose dedication to alcoholism research has been an inspiration; Robert D. Fink, MD, whose professional and personal friendship I consider invaluable; William D. Lerner, MD, whose enthusiasm for the alcohol and drug treatment process reversed a "burn-out" period in my career; Jack C. Morgan, MD, whose expertise in psychiatry has broadened my knowledge and enhanced my clinical skills; Susan Vaughn, whose continuing support as my executive secretary is absolutely essential for the completion of this book and other projects; Josephine Maddry, whose library research skills made this task enjoyable; Ed Stewart, whose non-medical advice, counsel, and support have been extraordinarily helpful; The Tennessee Department of Mental Health and Mental Retardation for initial and continuing administrative and financial support for alcoholism research at Memphis Mental Health Institute; The American Medical Association's Panel on Alcoholism — Manny Steindler, Joe Takamine, MD, Stanley Gitlow, MD, Le Clair Bissell, MD, Sheila Blume, MD, Robert Moore, MD, and Rogers Smith, MD — whose thoughtful deliberations concerning major and critical issues in the field of alcoholism have been exciting and reassuring to me; and to the late James H. Tharp, who established an Annual Research Award of which I was fortunate to be co-recipient.

Chapter 1
THE USE OF ALCOHOL: A MEDICAL PERSPECTIVE OF CRITICAL ISSUES

Historically, whenever any sociocultural milieu has been confronted with potentially destructive human behaviors that are difficult to understand and/or control, there are predictable responses. The first response is to pass laws against such behaviors; the second is to consider these behaviors as immoral or amoral; and the third response (perhaps when all else fails) is to designate the behaviors as a disease. When one uses a disease concept that is ill-defined in regard to etiology, natural history, diagnostic criteria, and treatment methodology, the tendency is to attach the suffix of "ism" or "ic" to the word or problem; thus, we have "alcoholism" and "alcoholic." The disease model of the personally and socially destructive use of ethyl alcohol is by no means a current concept. Attitudes of physicians toward alcoholism have varied considerably in the past; presently, these same variations cause concern, ambivalence, and confusion in the physician's attitudes toward the alcoholic person. Such variations in attitude include the concepts that:

- Alcoholic drinking is nothing more than excessive social drinking.
- Alcoholism is a self-inflicted "disease" caused by a lack of willpower.
- Alcoholism is a social problem, not a medical problem.
- Alcoholic drinking is a symptom of an underlying psychiatric illness.
- Treatment of the alcoholic person is futile because of the extremely poor prognosis.
- Alcoholism is the most treatable yet untreated illness in America today.
- Alcoholism is the most neglected health problem in the United States today and ranks with cancer and heart disease as a major threat to the nation's health.

It is little wonder that the physician may feel at a loss, both conceptually and functionally, when confronted with the responsibility of diagnosing and treating alcoholism and alcohol-related disorders. Although one often hears that physicians in the past (and, indeed, at present) have consciously avoided learning about and dealing directly with the alcoholic, medical science has

1

made significant contributions to our understanding of alcoholism and will continue to expand horizons in this field. However, as the field of medicine continues to develop better understanding of the phenomenon of alcoholism, consideration of a number of critical issues that can either obstruct or facilitate this process is essential. Among these critical issues are[1]: (a) definitional and diagnostic confusion concerning alcoholism; (b) the dilemma of alcohology as to who can and who should do what with the alcoholic person; (c) the question of "the best treatment approach" to the alcoholic person; (d) prognosis in terms of treatment outcome, that is "cure," "recovery," "remission," "relapse"; (e) the manifest differences between the alcohol dependencies in special populations, eg, adolescents, the elderly, women, blacks, American Indians, and Spanish Americans; and (f) treatment services—separation from or integration with the health care delivery system.

DEFINITIONAL AND DIAGNOSTIC CONFUSION CONCERNING ALCOHOLISM

The contemporary disease concept of alcoholism can be traced to the writings and experiences of Dr. Benjamin Rush, who in 1794 stated:

> The effects of ardent spirits divide themselves into such as are of a prompt and such as are of a chronic nature. The former discover themselves in drunkenness—an odious disease—and the latter in a numerous train of diseases and vices of the body and the mind.[2]

Although the disease states associated with excessive alcohol ingestion were originally dealt with by physicians, the disease concept per se has continued to be modified and amplified (even vilified) by medical and nonmedical disciplines. Nevertheless, many major organizations (eg, the American Medical Association (AMA); the American Medical Society on Alcoholism (AMSA); the National Council on Alcoholism (NCA); the American Psychiatric Association, and the American Academy of Family Practice have declared alcoholism a "disease." The implication of this concept for physicians is clear—theirs is the responsibility of diagnosis and treatment. In the practice of medicine, skillful and well-informed treatment is predicated on an adequate diagnosis. Although there have been numerous attempts to define the disease of alcoholism operationally and to gain consensual agreement among clinicians in this regard, there is no universal acceptance of extant diagnostic criteria; indeed, there is no consensus on whether or not alcoholism is a disease at all. In 1972, the National Council on Alcoholism published criteria for the diagnosis of alcoholism which include 28 major and 58 minor physiological, clinical, behavioral, psychological, and attitudinal parameters subdivided by diagnostic level of confidence.[3] These criteria are extremely useful, but have been criticized as being too cumbersome for the busy practitioner and because of the "overdiagnosis of alcoholism." Recently, the Diagnostic and Statistical Manual III (DSM III) of the American Psychiatric Association has published newer criteria for alcohol abuse, alcohol dependence (alcoholism), and other alcohol-related mental disorders.[4,5] These criteria will, in all probability, be accepted as standards for the diagnosis. However, these criteria are more behaviorally based and tend to ignore much of the available physiological information.

In attempting to resolve the social, psychological, and medical ambiguities of the term "alcoholism," the World Health Organization has taken a slightly different and, perhaps, more clinically useful diagnostic approach. In considering the consequences of excessive alcohol use, the physician must deal with *alcohol-dependence syndrome* as well as with *alcohol-related disabilities*.

In considering the single unitary *disease* concept of alcoholism, I have found a useful analogy—that of alcoholism and cancer.

Cancer is not a single disease, but represents many different disease states, having multiple etiologies and many different clinical manifestations. In addition, cancer is amenable to many different treatment approaches, has many different treatment outcomes, and is potentially fatal.

The same tenets apply to alcoholism, or rather to the alcoholisms or the alcohol-dependence syndrome. The alcohol-dependence syndrome (previously considered as alcoholism) is comprised of a group of disorders, at the core of which are tolerance to and a physical dependency on ethyl alcohol. The syndrome is of multidimensional origin and exists to varying degrees. The syndrome can be mild, moderate, or severe, intermittent or continuous, and can undergo clinical remission.

On the other hand, physicians are faced with a number of alcohol-related disabilities, which may or may not coexist with the alcohol-dependence syndrome. An alcohol-related disability is

> any difficulty in performance, which in accordance with the subject's age, sex and social role, involves activities which are accepted as basic concepts of daily living, such as self-care, social relations and economic activity—disability may be short-term, long-term or permanent.

The physician, in approaching alcohol-related pathology, should (a) determine whether or not the diagnosis of the alcohol-dependence syndrome exists; (b) operationally define the kinds and extent of concomitant disabilities; and (c) describe important physiological, psychological, social, and environmental factors which either exacerbate or ameliorate the alcohol-dependence syndrome and/or alcohol-related disabilities. This particular approach emphasizes that the alcohol-dependence syndrome and alcohol-related disabilities have multiple and different clinical presentations; thus, there is a need for multiple, differing and, it is hoped, disease-specific treatment interventions. The diagnosis of the alcohol-dependence syndrome (in regard to the alcoholisms) is of great importance and will be discussed in detail in subsequent chapters.

THE DILEMMA OF ALCOHOLOGY[6-8]

Although a few physicians since the time of Dr. Benjamin Rush have been leaders in the field of alcoholism, members of the medical profession can be considered recent newcomers to this area. The question of the proper person to deal most competently with alcohol problems is controversial. Should that person be the newly, specially trained medical professional (in this case, the practicing physician), or the person who has traditionally handled the problems (typified by the recovering or recovered alcoholic)? The medical professional assumes a clinical approach, which requires theory, empiricism, rationality, and freedom of investigation. Nonprofessional approaches to the treatment of alcoholism, most notable the Alcoholics Anonymous (AA) movement, have at times been viewed as dogmatic, restricting of investigation, and engaging in propagandistic dissemination of information. It would be counterproductive to dismiss, out-of-hand, the principles and results of this historical movement. However, we must be cognizant of the dilemma facing the physician in a clinical field (eg, alcohology) that claims to use scientific principles and theories in the service of helping the alcohol-dependent patient. How can the physician play a meaningful role in a climate in which research findings may be frequently ignored and disregarded?

If, in fact, the disease(s) model of alcohol dependence is accepted, it is incumbent on the physician to approach the problem in a scientific manner, while learning from the vast experience of the nonprofessional working in the field. Entry into this field of psychologists, social workers, nurses, and certified alcoholism counselors (including recovering and recovered alcoholics) is adding a new dimension to the scientific professional approach. Indeed, the trained and certified alcoholism counselor may be the most effective person to bridge the gap between science and craft. Further investigation and new research data will surely dramatically alter our concepts of diagnosis and treatment within the next decade and may lead to a closer alliance between the scientific professional and the nonprofessional workers.

THE BEST TREATMENT APPROACH

One potentially negative impact of the single unitary disease concept of alcoholism has been the search for, and at times the claim of, "the most effective treatment intervention." There are no existing data to support any presumption that one treatment is better than another. If one can appreciate the multidimensional nature of the alcohol-dependence syndrome and of alcohol-related disabilities, it is naive to restrict treatment concepts and approaches. The literature is rich with anecdotes; however, adequate evaluation studies comparing treatment modalities are sorely lacking. Review of different treatment modalities for alcoholism reveals that traditional treatment has changed very little during the past decade and that one approach offers little advantage over another, with one possible exception.[9,10] Treatment designed to alter or modify behaviors (not only drinking behavior but other maladaptive behaviors) may show the greatest promise for positive treatment outcomes. Physicians can play a critical role in the diagnosis and treatment of the alcohol-dependence syndrome.

PROGNOSIS IN TERMS OF TREATMENT OUTCOME

Many persons regard "alcoholism" as a chronic, progressive disease, from which a cure or recovery is never clinically realized; instead, they believe that a control (through abstinence from alcohol) of the disease is the only feasible prognostic expectation. Various claims that some "alcoholics" can return to a safe pattern of drinking have resulted in emotional and at times counterproductive rhetoric. The assertion is made that an "alcoholic" who resumes use of alcohol without attendant problems was not *really* an "alcoholic" in the first place. There are also a few reports which suggest that a certain (albeit small) percentage of "alcoholics" recover spontaneously with no treatment contact. These variations in outcome only tend to emphasize that we are probably dealing with many different types of alcoholisms, eg, the alcohol-dependence syndrome with or without concomitant alcohol-related disabilities.

Despite some of the methodological problems in its data collection, a document by the Rand Corporation should be scrutinized.[11] As the practicing physician contemplates the prognostic pessimism that still characterizes treatment of alcohol dependence, the following summary statements from the Rand Report may be helpful. The data were collected after four years on 85% of an original sample of 922 men admitted to eight federally supported alcoholism treatment centers in 1973. Of the sample, 54% were classified as problem drinkers (withdrawal symptoms, loss of control of alcohol ingestion, blackouts, alcohol-related illness, arrest, unemployment, and interpersonal problems). Of the sample, 46% were classified as being in "remission," that is, 28% were abstaining for the six-month period prior to data collection, and 18% were termed as persons who were "drinking without problems." The presence of alcohol-dependence symptoms (tolerance, withdrawal) after treatment significantly increased the probability of continuing drinking problems. However, provided that dependence was not present, the level of alcohol consumption did not appear to affect prognosis. The extent to which positive changes occurred could not be attributed to any particular treatment regimen, since significant improvement was observed in groups that had as little as a single contact with a treatment center.

It is obvious that there is still much to be learned about the natural history of alcohol-dependence syndrome; significant contributions are being and will be made by physicians who endeavor to diagnose and treat this syndrome.

MANIFEST DIFFERENCES BETWEEN ALCOHOL DEPENDENCIES IN SPECIAL POPULATIONS

Until recently, our concept of "the alcoholic" was based on information gathered on a Caucasian adult male (largely state hospital) patient population. In fact, a major criticism of the Rand Report referred to previously is that the outcome data derive from a male population. Within the past decade, clinical observations have raised critical questions: (a) Is alcohol dependency the same in men and women? (b) Is alcohol dependency the same in adults and in the young? (c) Is alcohol dependency the same in adults and the elderly? and (d) Is alcohol dependency the same among groups of differing racial and ethnic backgrounds? The answer to these questions is *NO*! We are beginning to discover important psychological, biological, and sociological differences in the etiology of, manifestations of, and treatment and recovery from alcohol-dependence syndrome between special populations. These differences present an even greater diagnostic and treatment challenge to the practicing physician.

TREATMENT SERVICES

The inaccessibility to treatment for the alcohol-dependent patient, recent legislative and judicial mandates concerning the management of the acute alcoholic, various federal funding patterns and the continuing confusion concerning the "disease concept" of alcoholism all tend to encourage the creation of a specialized but separate treatment system for alcoholics. This is not only counterproductive and fiscally infeasible, but also potentially therapeutically nihilistic. It is estimated that between 20% and 25% of all general hospital admissions and between 30% and 35% of all psychiatric admissions are directly or indirectly related to the use of ethyl alcohol; it becomes obvious that the major dimension of the "alcoholism iceberg" is still being ignored. A separate treatment system makes the diagnosis of alcoholism or the alcohol-dependence syndrome more exclusive and encourages health care professionals to continue diagnostic subterfuge, eg, "gastritis," "dehydration"; it also allows many major insurance providers to accept or reject claims arbitrarily. Failure to consider the role that alcohol plays in the pathogenesis of many medical, surgical, and psychiatric disorders that we treat is not consonant with quality health care. Specialized treatment programs are necessary as models for the treatment of alcohol-dependence syndrome, but these programs should be part of, not separate from, the existing health care delivery system. By integrating treatment services, health care issues can be clearly differentiated from social issues with regard to alcohol consumption; the medical scientist (physician) is seldom a social scientist, but is frequently seduced into confusing medical and social issues concerning alcoholism. A separate specialized treatment system that would probably at best exist tangentially to the health care delivery system only encourages this confusion. However, some positive factors currently in operation that are helping to resolve the separation-integration issue are: (a) improved training programs for medical students, physicians, and allied health professionals; (b) promulgation by the Joint Commission on Accreditation of Hospitals (JCAH) of standards for quality care for alcohol-dependent persons that embrace a philosophy of integration with rather than separation from the health care delivery system; and (c) willingness on the part of the health insurance industry to adopt a more realistic practice of reimbursement for quality care.

In developing an integrated treatment system, the physician should recognize the following important factors.[1,12]

Program Needs versus Client Needs

To define alcoholism as a disease with physiological, psychological, and sociocultural dysfunction (with both etiologic and consequential aspects) emphasizes the complexity and multiplicity of needs of the affected individual. Too often, treatment programs are designed that ignore the diversity of these needs and adhere more to the abilities and bias of the treatment staff. As a consequence, the needs of the program to succeed frequently transcend the meeting of needs of the patient. There are few, if any, existent programs that can afford total care without well-designed interdisciplinary cooperation.

Lack of Medical Involvement

Until recently, the exposure of medical students and physicians to alcoholism has involved the skid-row, chronic-court inebriate. Sociological issues are often inappropriately transformed into medical–psychiatric problems, leaving the practicing physician helpless, frustrated, and unable to appreciate the disease trajectory of alcoholism. Regardless of the controversy surrounding the disease concept of alcoholism, it is obvious that, as a drug, ethyl alcohol profoundly affects the public health. Involvement of physicians as diagnostic and treatment members of the "team" is essential in order to place this public health problem in proper perspective. The enthusiastic involvement of such organizations as the National Institute of Alcohol Abuse and Alcoholism (NIAAA), NCA, AMSA, and the AMA is slowly but effectively changing and shaping physicians' attitudes in this regard.

Therapeutic Territorial Imperatives

The community mental health center concept of geographically distinct "service areas" has created the "my patient" syndrome. Again, geography and competition for funding rather than patient needs often dictate the direction and quality of care. It is hoped that the procedure outlined by the JCAH and appropriately modified by many state authorities on alcoholism will dissolve these territorial imperatives and will again place administrative priorities secondary to health care priorities.

Separation: Alcoholism versus Drug Addiction versus Mental Illness

Although alcohol dependence is obviously the primary drug problem, the separation of planning, funding, and treatment approaches to alcohol dependence from those used for other drug problems (polydrug misuse is increasing) and further, the alienation of this area from the mental health concern creates an arbitrary division that discourages and denies recent advances in biological psychiatry. Although there are similarities and dissimilarities between these particular areas, the latter certainly does not obviate a more integrative approach, one demanding an expertise and a knowledge base for effective diagnosis and treatment. The idea of "alcoholism counselors," "drug addiction counselors," and "mental health counselors" ignores the overlap in these areas and is responsible for noncooperation, antagonism, and unnecessary competition. The loser is the patient. It is preferable that a treatment team be trained to deal with all these problems; this would encourage fiscal and program responsibility.

Inability to Apply Rational Authority

In a general sense, persons do not seek entrance into the health care delivery system unless they are "hurting," either psychologically or physically. Alcohol dependence, in a particular way, represents a behavioral disorder that often goes undetected at the personal level because of the denial and rationalization that are well-known diagnostic and therapeutic obstacles. In the opinion of many clinicians, it is essential to utilize rational authority (that is, external motivation or pragmatic coercion) as a means of assisting individuals to enter and remain in treatment. Alcohol-related job jeopardy, legal difficulties, or family and other interpersonal conflicts can be defined and used by the treatment team to modify drinking and other destructive aspects of the patient's behavior. Failure to modify behavior aggressively by the ethical and judicious use of rational authority frequently renders treatment programs impotent. The adage that an alcoholic cannot be helped until he is ready for help is often a tragic reflection on the inability or unwillingness to use coercive techniques. This involves interaction with the significant others in the patient's life (eg, employer, spouse, friends, etc) and emphasizing to the affected person the real or anticipated value loss that will occur if the behavioral problems of alcohol dependence continue.

Staffing Problems

The goal of meeting the patient's needs can only be accomplished by the "team approach," eg, utilizing the abilities of personnel with varied professional and nonprofessional backgrounds. Proper selection and training of staff is an obvious requirement. Development of a solidified but flexible and varied therapeutic esprit de corps is a necessary phenomenon in quality care. Ex-alcoholics or recovering alcoholics are not necessarily qualified candidates for a treatment team. Training of ex-alcoholic counselors according to the inherent direction of the program is essential. Nurturing of the staff with regard to developing a tolerance for recidivism decreases turnover and enhances the chances for continuity of care. It is important to expose treatment staff to "therapeutic successes," since exposure to recidivism and relapse is obvious. Defining responsibilities and limitations of members of a treatment staff prevents rescue fantasies that are detrimental to the patient and minimizes the "I am the most important person on the team" syndrome.

Lack of Proper Longitudinal Evaluation

Any treatment program must continue to ask the painful but essential question: "Is what we're doing better than nothing at all?" Follow-up evaluation with careful consideration of both therapeutic successes and therapeutic failures is difficult to develop; however, it is a mandatory effort for any treatment program that alleges to be flexible and effective.

Absence of a Heuristic Approach

Alcoholism research is not conducted only in well-funded centers directed by erudite investigators. On the contrary, all treatment programs have not only the opportunity but the responsibility to address the confused but still pertinent issues such as: definition of the disease of alcoholism; definition of individual response to treatment; definition of psychological and biological predictors that determine treatment plan; a search for predictors of success or failure; definition of proper treatment plans for individual patient needs; and definition of the determinants of spontaneous recovery from alcoholism, etc. A research attitude and atmosphere should permeate any effort in treating alcohol dependence.

Involvement of Treatment Personnel
with Policy and Decision Makers

The disruptive effect caused by alcohol misuse in our society attracts the attention of elected officials. Any responsible treatment program must encourage its members to be politically active in terms of influencing lawmakers and assisting them in drafting responsible legislation in order to separate, yet deal equally and effectively with, the sociocultural and the medical–psychiatric consequences of the use of alcohol. Retreat into the ivory tower of the health care delivery system invites uninformed but politically powerful intervention in the recognition and management of the public health problem of alcohol dependence.

Recognition of the historical reluctance and unwillingness of the physician to become more actively involved in the diagnosis and treatment of alcohol abuse/dependence has stimulated efforts to identify hypothetical reasons for this reluctance.[13] There are numerous such reasons. Persons with alcohol problems deny the dangers of their drinking patterns and refuse to discuss the matter with the physician. Although persons with alcohol problems recognize the dangers of the drinking pattern, they value their alcohol use more than their physiological, psychological, and social health, rejecting offers of treatment if they are made. They value their health and would like treatment, but are unwilling to cooperate when it is offered. Such persons tacitly accept offers of treatment and cooperate superficially but play the "alcoholic game" with their physicians and thereby provoke rejection.

Many physicians have either little or no training concerning persons with alcohol problems, or an "all or none" view of alcohol problems, thus either missing or ignoring all but the most severe cases. Often, they hold a moral rather than a medical view of alcohol problems; therefore, the patient is held solely responsible for recovery. In addition, many physicians believe that there is no effective treatment for alcohol problems and avoid the subject even when it is articulated by the patient. They may refuse to deal with alcohol and/or drugs with which they may be personally involved, or view the relapse in persons with alcohol problems as a therapeutic failure, eg, refusal to deal with the problem diminishes the risk of failure.

Although the above hypotheses may in part explain the physician's reluctance or unwillingness to deal with alcohol problems, recent evidence suggests that the responsibility for failure of early diagnosis and treatment is not solely due to either the physician or the patient, but derives from the role relationship between physician and patient. The person with an alcohol problem has great difficulty in assuming the submissive role of a patient, since accepting help impairs self-image and implies weakness in an individual who is otherwise engaged in a desperate power struggle with alcohol. The physician, who is not accustomed to having his or her authority challenged, raises a number of narcissistic defenses and retreats from diagnosis and treatment of the alcohol problem.

Regardless of the complex issues concerning the alcohol-dependence syndrome, the ubiquitous use of the drug ethyl alcohol in America today constitutes one of this nation's major health concerns, one which demands the creativity and skills of the practicing physician.

REFERENCES

1. Knott DH, Fink RD, Morgan JC: Development of a treatment system for alcoholism. *Alcoholism Digest* 4:vi–viii, 1976.
2. Rush B: An oration on the effects of spiritous liquors upon the human body. *American Museum* 4:325–327, 1788.
3. Criteria Committee of the National Council on Alcoholism: Criteria for the Diagnosis of Alcoholism. *Am J Psychiatry* 129:127–135, 1972.
4. Spitzer R, Sheehy M: DSM III: A classification system in development. *Psychiatr Ann* 6:102–109, 1976.
5. *Diagnostic and Statistical Manual of Mental Disorders*, ed 3. The American Psychiatric Association, pp 163–171, 1980.
6. Kalb M, Propper MS: The future of alcohology: Craft or science? *Am J Psychiatry* 133:641–645, 1976.
7. Davis TA, Knott DH: The dilemma of alcohology. *Kentucky Alcoholism Council Newsletter* 5:7–9, 1978.
8. Knott DH: Alcoholism and drug abuse: Whose territory? *Frontiers Psychiatry* 10:11–13, 1980.
9. Pattison EM: Ten years of change in alcoholism treatment and delivery systems. *Am J Psychiatry* 134:261–266, 1977.
10. Sobell MB, Sobell LC: The aftermath of heresy: A response to Pendery et al.'s (1982) critique of "Individualized behavior therapy for alcoholics." *Behav Res Ther* 22:413–440, 1984.
11. Polich JM, Armor DJ, Braiker HB: Patterns of alcoholics over four years. *J Stud Alcohol* 41:396–416, 1980.
12. Knott, DH, Fink RD: Problems surrounding emergency care services for acute alcoholism. *Hosp Community Psychiatry* 26:42–43, 1975.
13. Imhof J, Hirsch R, Terenzi RD: Countertransferential and attitudinal considerations in the treatment of drug abuse and addiction. *J Substance Abuse Treatment* 1:21–30, 1984.

Chapter 2
THE DRUG, ETHYL ALCOHOL: SOME BIOCHEMICAL ASPECTS

Most physicians view alcohol as a drug, yet alcohol is still viewed as a food with some significant nutritive value. Although some physicians still prescribe alcohol for either its nutritive or "psychic" benefits, the preponderance of information indicates that alcohol is of little value, either as a "prescription" drug or a food. In fact, if alcohol could only be obtained by prescription, it would probably be unavailable, eg, its toxicity and potential for dependence are too great.

METABOLISM OF ALCOHOL[1-5]

Approximately 80% to 90% of ingested alcohol is metabolized via a pathway involving alcohol dehydrogenase (ADH). Small amounts of ADH can be found in the kidney and gastric mucosa; most of the ADH is hepatic, the liver being the primary site for the metabolism of alcohol.

Alcohol dehydrogenase catalyzes the following reaction:

Ethanol (C_2H_5OH) + nicotine adenine dinucleotide (NAD) $\rightleftarrows$ acetaldehyde (CH_3CHO) + NADH + H.

One of the critical metabolic factors is the generation of excessive amounts of NADH. Ninety percent of acetaldehyde is metabolized in the liver, the process catalyzed by the aldehyde dehydrogenase system, to acetate, and ultimately through the citric acid cycle to CO_2 and H_2O. It has been suggested that many of the toxic effects of ethyl alcohol are actually due to acetaldehyde, and differential rates of elimination of this substance may exist between "alcoholics" and "nonalcoholics."

Non-ADH pathways for alcohol metabolism have been demonstrated, but the clinical significance of these await further elucidation. In studies concerning the development of tolerance to alcohol a number of basic experiments (in vivo and in vitro) have suggested the existence of non-ADH mechanisms for alcohol metabolism.

Microsomal Ethanol Oxidizing System (MEOS)

Chronic experimental alcohol use leads to a hypertrophy of the smooth endoplasmic reticulum in the liver, suggesting an increase in enzyme activity associated with the breakdown of alcohol. It has been found that an increase in the oxidation of ethanol by isolated microsomes is present:

$$NADPH + H^+ + O_2 + \text{alcohol } (C_2H_5OH) \rightarrow CH_3CHO \text{ (acetaldehyde)} + NADP^+ + 2H_2O.$$

Catalase

Catalase, which is found in the perioxisomes, mitochondria, and microsomes of the hepatocyte is capable of oxidizing ethanol in vitro in the presence of a system that generates hydrogen peroxide (H_2O_2):

$$\text{Catalase } H_2O_2 + C_2H_5OH \text{ (alcohol)} \rightarrow \text{Catalase} + CH_3CHO \text{ (acetaldehyde)} + 2H_2O.$$

Although there has been considerable controversy concerning the roles played by MEOS or the catalase system in altering the rates of alcohol metabolism, there are insufficient data in this regard to warrant any clinically useful assumptions at this point.

Frequently overlooked when the medical complications of alcohol use are considered is the phenomenon of incredibly large doses even in nonproblem drinkers. Indeed, the dosage is usually so high (in both the acute and chronic situation) that the metabolic systems responsible for the degradation and elimination of alcohol are "overloaded," leading to a number of metabolic disturbances which contribute to the pathophysiology observed.

To understand the dosage issue better, it should be emphasized that alcohol distributes throughout the total body water and can affect the metabolism in all cells of the body, with the rate of alcohol metabolism in a man weighing 70 kg approximating 100 mg/kg per hour, or 7 g/h. In 1.5 ounces of beverage alcohol, the amount of ethyl alcohol consumed is: (a) 80 proof (40% vol/vol) 14.3 g; (b) 86 proof (43% vol/vol) 15.3 g; (c) 100 proof (50% vol/vol) 17.9 g; (d) 1 bottle of domestic beer (3.6% vol/vol) 10.3 g.

After alcohol is ingested, blood alcohol concentration (BAC) reaches a peak and then decreases by 0.21 mg/100mL/kg per hour. This is of practical as well as theoretical importance, since the biotransformation process of alcohol elimination exhibits zero-order kinetics (eg, the rate of elimination is constant) at an alcohol concentration produced by the ingestion of very small quantities of ethanol. It is obvious that the human metabolic system for handling even small doses of alcohol (eg, 1.5 oz of 80 proof = 14.3 g) is not too efficient, leading to a number of biochemical consequences.

Many of these consequences result from the fact that only 2% to 10% of ingested alcohol is excreted through the kidney and lungs; 90% to 98% is oxidized in the body, the principal site being the liver. As indicated previously the NADH/NAD ratio changes dramatically with the metabolism of alcohol, eg, the augmented transfer of hydrogen to NAD. This ratio changes the metabolites, which are dependent on a normal NADH/NAD ratio, leading to a number of abnormalities. Clinically significant abnormalities include altered carbohydrate metabolism (decreased gluconeogenesis, hypoglycemia, labile glucostatic mechanism) and increased lactate-pyruvate ratio resulting in hyperlacticacidemia. The hyperlacticacidemia in turn results in acidosis, increases the tendency toward ketosis, and decreases the renal secretion of uric acid; the resulting hyperuricemia can be symptomatic by precipitating a gouty attack. An altered NADH/NAD ratio increases hepatic lipogenesis. Indeed, many types of clinical pathology secondary to acute and chronic excessive alcohol ingestion result from the enhanced formation and deposition of lipids in various tissues (eg, fatty liver, cardiomyopathy). Chronic alcohol consumption also impairs the absorption, assimilation, production, and biotransformation of protein.

Although there is further investigation needed in the area of alcohol and nutrition (especially lower doses of alcohol) and although most of the conclusions in this regard are based on studies of "chronic alcoholics" and of experimental efforts making use of large doses of alcohol, it is difficult to defend the premise that alcohol is a "food" or that it has any nutritive value.

Remembering that 1.5 oz of 80 proof (40% vol/vol) beverage alcohol contains 14.3 g of alcohol, it is important to realize that each gram of ethanol provides 7.1 calories. Thus, 239 mL (10 oz) of 80 proof alcohol represents 670 calories, or approximately one fourth to one third of the daily caloric requirement. Beverage alcohol contains insufficient amounts of protein, vitamins, and minerals; thus, the calories derived from alcohol have been termed "naked" or "empty" calories. Replacement of useful calories with alcohol calories exacerbates metabolic problems. However, the concept that a nutritious diet with vitamin supplements will permit a person to drink as much alcohol as desired without detriment to health is a myth. A nutritious diet, plus vitamins, plus the chronic excessive ingestion of ethanol can still produce significant metabolic derangements, the same disease states seen in the "malnourished" alcoholic.

Because ingestion and metabolism of alcohol involve a large caloric load (sometimes at the expense of other nutrients), insignificant amounts of extra hepatic excretion, primary oxidation in the liver with adverse metabolic effects, and no storage mechanism in the body, it is essential that we cease to regard alcohol as a *food* and regard ethanol as a potentially *toxic* sedative–hypnotic drug, which we frequently consume in far more massive doses than the other commonly used sedative agents.

TOLERANCE

Tolerance is the need for increased dosages of alcohol to produce the desired central nervous system (CNS) effect or, if the dosage of alcohol remains constant, the gradual attenuation of CNS effects of alcohol with repeated exposures to the drug.[6,7]

Tolerance is the biological phenomenon that is probably responsible for most of the consequential psychopathology and pathophysiology observed in alcohol-dependence syndrome. Unfortunately, tolerance to the toxic effects of alcohol does not parallel the tolerance developed to the CNS effects of ethanol. Although our knowledge of opiate tolerance has been enhanced by extensive investigation, that paradigm (eg, specifically of drug–receptor interaction) cannot explain fully the mechanisms of tolerance to alcohol. In light of our current understanding, well-defined receptor mechanisms specific to alcohol do not appear to exist.

Two mechanisms are commonly offered to explain the clinical phenomenon of tolerance: metabolic tolerance and CNS adaptation. Human studies have demonstrated that, to a slight degree, the rates of ethanol metabolism may increase as a function of amount and duration of alcohol ingestion in alcoholics. This may be a reflection of the increase in the oxidation of ethanol by the microsomal ethanol-oxidizing system; it is less likely that an increase in the catalase system plays a role. However, further studies reveal that there is no significant difference between the rate of alcohol metabolism between alcoholic and nonalcoholic persons after a three-week period of abstinence from ethanol. No data clearly support the assumption that continual use of ethanol contributes significantly to development of tolerance by enhancement of alcohol metabolism.

CNS Cellular Adaptation

Alcohol diffuses freely in total body water, and the concentration of alcohol in any portion of the CNS is dependent on the water concentration of the cells involved. The mechanisms by which these cells "adapt" to repeated exposures to alcohol are speculative yet intriguing, and certainly have research implications concerning possible prevention of or at least amelioration of tolerance, which in turn might reduce the toxicity associated with large doses of alcohol. It is thought that alcohol is accompanied by an increased cholesterol content and a change in fatty acid composition of cells of the CNS. These changes may hinder the movement of alcohol from the extracellular space; only by increasing the extracellular concentration of alcohol can this obstacle be overcome and the intracellular effect of alcohol be perceived. Alcohol may cause a redistribution of CA^{2+} ions in cell membranes in certain portions of the brain. A similar response can be observed with opiates and may represent a common mechanism involved with drug tolerance. It is also possible that certain CNS cells chronically exposed to alcohol exhibit a reduction in general receptor sites, as indicated by a decrease in N-demethylating enzymes. Furthermore, it is postulated that alcohol interferes with essential CNS physiological functions that are under feedback control. Alcohol reduces this physiological function resulting in a decrease in feedback control, which in turn leads to a compensating increase in activity. This increase offsets the effect of the drug, ie, tolerance.

Tolerance Factors

The hypotheses explaining tolerance to alcohol are speculative and vague; however, current research efforts in this area may produce clinically useful information in the near future. There are some factors concerning tolerance to alcohol that are clinically relevant.

Etiologic Mechanisms

Acute tolerance to alcohol develops with one drinking episode. If one measures impairment in certain psychomotor performance tests during the rising and falling phases of the blood alcohol curve, more impairment exists at a given BAC (eg, .04) when the blood alcohol is rising than at the same concentration (eg, .04) when the blood alcohol is falling. It is not known if the same etiologic mechanisms are operational for acute tolerance as for chronic tolerance.

Rate of Development

The rate of development of alcohol tolerance is dependent not only on the mean daily dose of alcohol, but on how rapidly the alcohol is consumed. In other words, the chronic daily ingestion of a pint of distilled spirits within a period of two hours will result in a more rapid rate of development and a greater degree of tolerance than if the pint of distilled spirits was consumed daily but over a period of six hours.

Redevelopment

Once tolerance to alcohol has developed and then is allowed to disappear with cessation of alcohol intake, it is reacquired more rapidly with successive cycles of alcohol intake.

Tolerance–dependence

Tolerance to and physical dependence on alcohol are closely related and develop in parallel in humans; thus, the greater the degree of tolerance, the greater the degree of physical dependence.

Cross-tolerance

If tolerance to alcohol exists, there is a cross-tolerance observed to other sedative–hypnotics and general anesthetics. In all probability, an enhanced metabolism of these and other drugs plays no significant role in cross-tolerance. Although the exact mechanism is unknown, there are well-recognized clinical problems associated with cross-tolerance, such as the necessity to use larger than usual doses of sedatives and anesthetics to achieve desired effects.

Aging Process

The ability in humans to develop tolerance to alcohol is in part a function of age; after age 40 years, this ability continually declines with the aging process.

BACs

The distinct yet global impairment of CNS functions produced by alcohol is manifest at BACs well below those concentrations required to affect excitability, impulse conduction, and transmitter release by the CNS cell.

Because tolerance to alcohol is fundamental to the diagnosis of the alcohol-dependence syndrome (alcoholism), it is imperative that research efforts continue to search for the basic biological mechanisms involved. Further knowledge in this area will not only make the diagnostic approach more sophisticated, but might also allow us some day to alter the course and even the onset of alcoholism as it is currently operationally defined.

PHYSICAL DEPENDENCE

Physical dependence is the onset of withdrawal signs and symptoms following the abrupt cessation or a marked reduction in the use of alcohol.[8,9] As with tolerance, the existence of physical dependence is fundamental to the diagnosis of alcohol dependence syndrome (alcoholism). Historically, it was assumed that alcohol withdrawal signs and symptoms resulted from an intercurrent illness and/or specific nutritional deficiencies, and that withdrawal occurred only after long periods of regular and excessive alcohol ingestion resulted in a high degree of tolerance. It is now appreciated that physical dependence can occur after brief exposures to alcohol (even after one drink) and that our understanding of a clinically significant withdrawal state depends on: (a) criteria for withdrawal symptoms; (b) sensitivity of techniques used to detect withdrawal phenomena; and (c) the rate at which the drug (alcohol) is removed from its site of action.

The hypotheses explaining the pathogenesis of physical dependence on alcohol are legion and closely parallel the explanations for the development of tolerance.

Withdrawal Syndrome

Figure 2.1 (schematic) illustrates the withdrawal state from alcohol (physical dependence). The depressant effect of alcohol on CNS function is maximal when BAC peaks; thereafter, a rebound hyperexcitability begins to develop, with a decreasing BAC, and persists for a period of time after the BAC reaches zero. This rebound hyperexcitability is the withdrawal syndrome, and its intensity varies from being very mild (insomnia) to being fatal (delirium, convulsions). Important to the reliable diagnosis of alcohol dependence syndrome is a consensual agreement on what constitutes a clinically significant withdrawal syndrome reflective of physical dependency, since, as stated previously, one can demonstrate, and indeed experience, mild withdrawal after one drink of alcohol.

The rebound hyperexcitability following use of alcohol probably involves the entire neuroaxis, with the reticular activating system being more sensitive

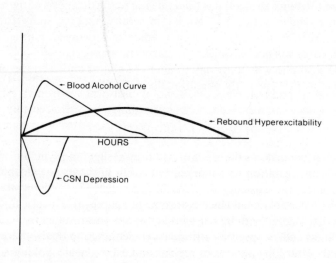

Figure 2.1. Sedative–agitating effect of alcohol.

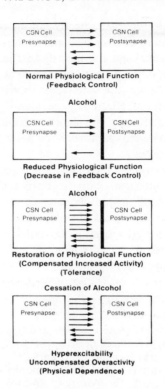

Figure 2.2. Feedback control: tolerance and physical dependence.

to the effects of alcohol withdrawal than are cortical structures. The basis for this hyperexcitability may be the compensating increase in feedback activity continuing as an uncompensated overactivity unopposed by the drug effect (Fig. 2.2).

Some physical dependence factors may prove to have clinical relevance (eg, the diagnosis and treatment of alcohol withdrawal syndrome). Alcohol ingestion leads to an increase in CNS intracellular Na^+; conceivably, transcellular membrane potential could thus be decreased, causing an increased sensitivity of the cell membrane to both exogenous and endogenous stimuli.

Alcohol use decreases total exchangeable magnesium, the Mg^{2+} ion normally exerts a quieting effect on neural tissue. In addition, alcohol use and cessation of its use results in an increase in circulating levels of catecholamines.

Signs of physical dependence are acquired more rapidly with repeated exposures to alcohol. The relationship between compulsive alcohol use and physical dependency on alcohol is variable and complex. Because physical dependence (withdrawal phenomena) technically can exist after one drink of alcohol, it is highly questionable whether physical dependency per se causes compulsive alcohol use. Rather than directly causing compulsive use, physical dependence contributes to its development and to the tendency to relapse after withdrawal. Generally speaking, the severity of the withdrawal symptoms varies with (a) intensity, and (b) the duration of the preceding exposure to alcohol. However, one cannot always assume that the severity or extent of physical dependency is totally reflected by the intensity of the withdrawal syndrome since the latter is affected and significantly influenced by a number of variables, among which are age, associated pathophysiologic states, and concomitant psychopathology.

The clinical relevance of these factors will be explored in greater detail in the following chapter, which deals with diagnosis and treatment of the acute phase of alcohol abuse and alcohol dependence syndrome.

It is apparent that the biological phenomena of tolerance and physical dependence, so crucial to the diagnosis of alcohol dependence syndrome, also create a clinical challenge to the physician in regard to skillful and well-informed treatment approaches.

REFERENCES

1. Kalant H: Absorption, diffusion, distribution, and elimination of ethanol: Effects of biological membranes, in Kissin B, Begleiter H (eds): *The Biology of Alcoholism: I, Biochemistry*. New York, Plenum, 1971, pp 1–46.
2. Von Wartzburg JP: The metabolism of alcohol in normals and alcoholics: Enzymes, in Kissin B, Begleiter H (eds): *The Biology of Alcoholism: I, Biochemistry*. New York, Plenum, 1971, pp 63–91.
3. Truitt EB, Walsh MJ: The role of acetaldehyde in the actions of ethanol, in Kissin B, Begleiter H (eds): *The Biology of Alcoholism: I, Biochemistry*. New York, Plenum, 1971, pp 161–187.
4. Tewari S, Carson VG: Biochemistry of alcohol and alcohol metabolism, in Pattison EM, Kaufman E (eds): *Encyclopedic Handbook of Alcoholism*. New York, Gardner, 1982, pp 83–105.
5. Erickson CK: Factors affecting the distribution and measurement of alcohol in the body, in Majchrowics E, Noble E (eds): *Biochemistry and Pharmacology of Ethanol*. New York, Plenum, 1979, pp 9–23.
6. Mendelson JH: Biochemical mechanisms of alcohol addiction, in Kissin B, Begleiter H (eds): *The Biology of Alcoholism: I, Biochemistry*. New York, Plenum, 1971, pp 513–540.
7. Kissin B: Theory and practice in the treatment of alcoholism, in Kissin B, Begleiter H (eds): *The Biology of Alcoholism: V, Treatment and Rehabilitation of the Chronic Alcoholic*. New York, Plenum, 1977, pp 1–51.
8. Gitlow SE: An overview in alcoholism, in Gitlow SE, Peyser HS (eds): *Alcoholism: A Practical Treatment Guide*. Orlando, Fla, Grune & Stratton, 1980, pp 1–22.
9. Gross MM (ed): *Alcohol Intoxication and Withdrawal: Experimental Studies: XXXV, Advances in Experimental Medicine and Biology*. New York, Plenum, 1973.

Chapter 3
ALCOHOL ABUSE AND ALCOHOL DEPENDENCE: ACUTE PHASE

Legislative and judicial attention became critically focused on the acute phase of alcohol dependence syndrome (alcoholism) in the mid-1960s. The basic issue addressed was whether or not the management of the public inebriate should be the responsibility of law enforcement or of the health care system, with decisions and mandates favoring the latter approach. These mandates, in conjunction with increased reimbursement for care from public and private sources, the promulgation of standards of care by the Joint Commission on Accreditation of Hospitals (JCAH), and the nascent public acceptance of the disease concept of alcoholism, have sensitized the health care delivery system, and in particular the primary care physician, to the prevalence and seriousness of alcohol abuse and alcohol dependence in the acute form as well as in the subacute and chronic forms.[1]

The implied altruistic intent of mandatory health care rather than incarceration for the public inebriate has created a number of questions and problems for the practicing physician, who must decide on the best approach to the diagnosis and triaging of medical–psychiatric problems associated with alcohol intoxication and withdrawal reactions. The physician must also determine the most rational treatment approach and whether there is indeed a standardized, well-accepted treatment strategy. Further questions to be resolved are whether acute alcoholics require medication, how effectively such patients can be managed in a nonmedical setting, and whether any predictors exist that can assist the physician in forecasting a more serious form of alcohol withdrawal?

The acute phase of alcohol dependence syndrome includes the periods of intoxication and withdrawal. Contrary to some opinions, many persons suffering the acute phase can be managed on an outpatient basis, often in a nonmedical setting.[2] However, the primary care physician is increasingly confronted with patients suffering the acute phase of alcohol dependence and can significantly contribute to their recovery with conservative yet skillful treatment, with the provision of medical–psychiatric support services for more

21

difficult cases. Although treatment of the acute phase is often the "easiest" aspect of management, important initial ingredients in the overall long-term treatment of these patients include their physiological rehabilitation and the amelioration of the morbidity associated with the acute phase, ie, detoxification.

EPIDEMIOLOGICAL CONSIDERATIONS[3]

Consumption Level and Severity of Symptoms

The frequency of more severe forms of alcohol abstinence syndrome (alcohol withdrawal delirium) correlates with an increase in consumption of distilled spirits; the frequency of alcohol withdrawal delirium decreases when beer is consumed in relative preference to distilled spirits.

Socioeconomic Status

Until recently, the likelihood in this country of an individual's being admitted to a medical facility for detoxication correlated directly with the coexistence of unemployment, low income, low educational achievement, multiple arrests for alcohol-related behaviors, and receipt of welfare payments. However, as intervention opportunities have increased, particularly with employee-assistance programs, the stereotype noted above has been altered dramatically. Persons who are employed, who have intact families, and who have achieved higher levels of education are being admitted to medical facilities for detoxication. Furthermore, as the credibility of the disease concept of alcohol dependence increases, many patients who were detoxified under the guise of "gastritis," "anxiety," "depression," etc are now diagnosed more appropriately as suffering from alcohol dependence.

Duration of Use

The duration of excessive alcohol use is also a factor: Patients with a history of heavy drinking of less than ten years' duration were less likely to experience alcohol withdrawal delirium than were those with greater than a ten-year history. However, if the alcohol dependence syndrome occurs after the age of 40 years, this latency period of ten years is significantly reduced.

Sex Ratio

In the past, men have outnumbered women 4 to 1 in groups admitted for the treatment of alcohol withdrawal delirium. This may be due to a different visibility of men and women who are alcohol-dependent, or possibly to a difference in alcohol metabolism between the sexes. It is anticipated that as more attention is focused on target populations (in this case, women) this sex ratio will decrease.

Recurrence Rate

There is evidence suggesting that the recurrence rate of alcohol withdrawal delirium in this country approximates 43%; this may be an important predictor in the triaging process. It is probable that both physiological as well as psychosocial factors contribute to a high recurrence rate.

TERMINOLOGY

The following discussion will focus on the acute phase from these aspects[4-7]: (a) mild, moderate, and severe alcohol intoxication; (b) alcohol abstinence (withdrawal) syndrome; and (c) toxic psychoses associated with either intoxication or withdrawal, including idiosyncratic (pathological) intoxication, hallucinosis, alcohol amnestic syndrome, paranoid state, and dementia.

Alcohol Intoxication: Diagnosis and Treatment

The mild signs and symptoms of alcohol intoxication include: impaired judgment, emotional lability, and nystagmus (particularly horizontal nystagmus with lateral gaze. Moderate symptoms include dilated pupils that are slowly reactive to light; dysarthria (slurred speech); dysmetria (improper measuring of distance); ataxia; and wide-based staggering gait. Severe symptoms are convulsions, coma and death.

The degree of impairment produced by alcohol is a function of the blood alcohol concentration (BAC) and the rate at which intoxicating levels were achieved and the duration of intoxication. It is important to remember that a given BAC will produce more impairment in adolescents and the elderly than in the adult population.

Although seizures occur more frequently during obvious alcohol withdrawal, high blood alcohol levels can be associated with convulsions, particularly as the BAC begins to decline.

It is unusual to encounter coma due only to alcohol in the adult population, but it occurs more frequently in children, adolescents, and the geriatric population.

Although tolerance to alcohol develops with regard to the behavioral manifestations of intoxication, there may not be a concomitant increase in tolerance to the lethal dose, so that severe acute intoxication may be superimposed on chronic intoxication at any time. When alcohol alone produces coma, death may result from respiratory depression. However, if coma is present at a BAC of < 0.35 (350 mg/dl) the physician should suspect associated complications. The more common complications include head and spinal cord injuries, hypoglycemia, diabetic coma, hepatic coma, hemodynamically significant cardiac arrhythmia, a generalized or partial seizure, and overdose in combination with other drugs. In fact, coma associated with acute alcohol intoxication must be presumed to be secondary to alcohol combined with other potentially life-threatening complications.

With severe forms of alcohol intoxication, it is important to correlate the clinical signs with the BAC. However, in many areas laboratories are not able to ascertain blood alcohol levels immediately. A useful and convenient parameter to substitute is the serum or plasma osmolality, which yields a "guesstimate" of the BAC.[8] Alcohol exerts a definite osmotic effect, dependent on its concentration. One can assume that the normal baseline plasma or serum osmolality in the nonintoxicated state is 290 mOsm/kg H_2O. An alcohol-induced increase of 23 mOsm/kg H_2O above the baseline value of 290 correlates with a BAC of 0.1 or 100 mg/dL. Thus, if a patient has alcohol on the breath, and is in coma with a plasma osmolality of 313 (290 + 23 = 313), the BAC probably approximates 0.1, and an immediate search for additional causes of the coma should be instituted. If the same patient had a plasma osmolality of 328 mOsm/kg H_2O or above (290 + 92 = 382), the calculated BAC would be 0.4 (400 mg/dL); the blood alcohol level would be playing a more major role in the genesis of the coma.

Humans have been getting drunk and sobering up for thousands of years without benefit of hospitals, physicians, nurses, or medication. Alcohol is rapidly metabolized at a rate of approximately 15 mg/dL per hour (range 15 mg/dL per hour to 22 mg/dL per hour); this normal detoxification process usually occurs without medical intervention and without serious complications.

Treatment of Mild Intoxication

Treatment of mild intoxication is a combination of skillful neglect (no medication) and observation of the subject for emergence of withdrawal symptoms.

Treatment of Moderate Intoxication

Treatment of moderate intoxication involves observation of the subject for emergence of withdrawal symptoms; encouragement of nutrition; administration of thiamine 100 mg p.o. or intramuscularly; and, possibly, administration of 1,000 mL of fructose (10%) IV.

The approach to moderate intoxication has been characterized by a rather passionate search for "sobering up" (amethystic) agents. Attempts to use caffeine (and other stimulants), steroids, thyroxine, triiodothyronine, epinephrine, insulin, and insulin plus glucose have failed to increase the rate of alcohol metabolism. Some clinicians have used fructose on the basis that the conversion of fructose to glucose in the liver is associated with a slight increase in the rate of alcohol removal. However, large doses of fructose are thought to cause (or exacerbate) gastrointestinal disturbances, metabolic (lactic) acidosis, and hyperuricemia. We have found, in selected, moderately intoxicated hospitalized patients, that the IV administration of 1,000 mL of 10% fructose did not cause any obvious adverse effects and appeared to "sober up" the patient more rapidly. This impression is obviously anecdotal; if the choice to use fructose is made, the patient should be observed very closely, and the physician should recognize that the alleged amethystic effect of fructose is controversial.

Treatment of Severe Intoxication

If the subject is comatose or in a semicomatose condition, support ventilation mechanically; search for and treat the causes of coma; correct fluid, electrolyte, and acid-base disturbances; administer thiamine 100 mg intramuscularly; and consider peritoneal dialysis or hemodialysis for BACs of 0.6 (600 mg/dL) or greater. In addition, perform gastric lavage and administer activated charcoal if this can be performed within two hours of the consumption of large amounts of alcohol. Take precautions against seizures, and observe for the emergence of withdrawal symptoms. Do not use analeptics (caffeine, amphetamines, methylphenidate [Ritalin]) to stimulate the patient because these agents may cause seizures and cardiovascular disturbances. Coma associated with alcohol intoxication is a life-threatening emergency and should be treated in a medical intensive-care setting.

Although alcohol intoxication can occasionally pose a serious threat to the patient, the alcohol abstinence (withdrawal) syndrome is more responsible for the morbidity and mortality associated with the acute phase of alcohol dependence syndrome.

Alcohol Abstinence (Withdrawal) Syndrome

Figure 3.1 illustrates the augmenting effect of repeated doses of alcohol on the rebound hyperexcitability phenomenon. The sedative effect of alcohol is relatively short-term, whereas the augmenting effect is of lower amplitude but longer duration. The cumulative effect of repeated doses of alcohol results in clinically significant forms of alcohol abstinence (withdrawal) syndrome.[9]

Stages

The nosology of this syndrome continues to be plagued by such terms as "mild DTs," "impending DTs," and "incipient DTs." A useful descriptive approach to alcohol abstinence syndrome, originally defined in 1813 and later modified, divides this disorder into distinct but overlapping stages.[5] Stage I

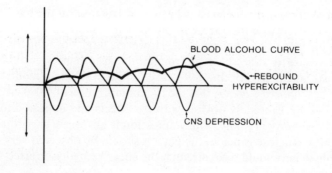

Figure 3.1. Relationship between short-term, sedative effect of ethanol and its long-term agitating effect.

consists of psychomotor agitation; autonomic hyperactivity consisting of hypertension, tachycardia, diaphoresis; anorexia; insomnia; and illusions. Stage I can begin at any time that the BAC begins to decrease up until 72 to 96 hours after the last drink; most frequently, the onset of stage I begins within 12 to 36 hours after the last drink. Often stage I is self-limiting and will last from a few hours to one to two days, depending on the intensity and duration of the precedent exposure to alcohol. However, if abstinence syndrome progresses, stage II follows.

Stage II consists of stage I symptoms with the addition of hallucinations of auditory, visual, tactile, and olfactory (rare) nature. Typically the hallucinations are of a mixed variety and are usually threatening, leading to paranoid ideations and behavior. There may be partial or total amnesia of the hallucinatory experience (frequently a family member, friend, or nurse, etc, observes this phenomenon), but when questioned later, the patient may deny experiencing hallucinations. The hallucinations may be transient and intermittent.

Increasing morbidity and mortality is observed with progression to stage III, consisting of stage I and stage II symptoms with the addition of disorientation, delusions, and delirium. It is relatively rare that an acute patient progresses to stage III unless there are concomitant complicating conditions. There may be seizure activity. In some instances, a seizure (usually generalized — grand mal) will precede and perhaps precipitate the onset of psychotic symptoms (stage II and stage III). Other factors include: infection — especially respiratory tract infections; associated trauma; hypoglycemia; multiple drug dependencies — especially alcohol and other sedative–hypnotics; and pancreatitis.

A patient suffering from stage III withdrawal (which can legitimately be called delirium tremens) generally has an associated medical–surgical disorder which must be diagnosed and treated if there is to be a favorable prognosis.

Alcohol Withdrawal Seizures

In some cases of severe withdrawal, a generalized seizure precedes the onset of stages II and III. More frequently, however, the alcohol withdrawal seizure can occur de novo and in an isolated situation, without consequent exacerbation of withdrawal symptoms. The alcohol withdrawal seizure usually occurs within a period beginning with a decrease in BAC and extending up to 72 to 96 hours after the last drink. The seizure is usually generalized (but partial seizures can occur) and is self-limiting; only occasionally will status epilepticus be encountered. Contributing factors for the alcohol withdrawal seizure are multiple: (a) respiratory alkalosis secondary to hyperventilation with elevation in arterial and cerebrospinal fluid lactate, decreased serum magnesium, increased pH, and decreased pCO_2 occurs; (b) transcellular membrane potential is altered due to an accumulation of Na^+ intracellularly secondary to the effects of alcohol; and (c) a rapidly decreasing blood sugar level–hypoglycemia. If a true alcohol withdrawal seizure occurs, it is important to remember that long-term anticonvulsant therapy is not warranted although if the patient suffers alcohol withdrawal syndrome in the future, seizures are more likely to recur. Intravenous diazepam appears to be the drug of choice in controlling a seizure. Intravenous Dilantin should be used with *extreme* caution since this treatment has been associated with serious ventricular tachyarrhythmias.

Following an alcohol withdrawal seizure, neurological evaluation of the subject is usually normal. If a seizure occurs after 96 hours (after the last drink), one must consider another basic epileptogenic process such as posttraumatic seizures, idiopathic epilepsy, severe metabolic disturbances, etc.

Although the staging process described above has usefulness in the medical setting, there has been increasing interest recently in formalizing the management of persons suffering alcohol withdrawal syndrome in nonmedical treatment settings. There are four reasons why needless controversy over medical *v* nonmedical treatment of the acute phase exists. First, many persons suffering alcohol withdrawal never progress past stage I and suffer only mild discomfort; these persons recover rapidly in a supportive environment and require no medication for control. Second, the nonmedical setting is usually more cost-effective to operate. Third, many persons seen in hospital emergency rooms for detoxication can be handled in a less restrictive environment. Fourth, although it is unfortunate, there exists no universally accepted triage procedure to assist the care provider in determining the level of intervention required for the treatment of the alcohol withdrawal syndrome. We have recently modified a symptom evaluation scale that is designed to yield an objective score, can be used for initial evaluation, and can be used by medical and trained nonmedical personnel alike.[10] This clinical evaluation system consists of 30 clinical variables with specific operationally defined quantitative scales (see Appendix, Abstinence Symptom Evaluation Scale ASE Scale). With this scale, there are three scores to be ascertained: *total score, selected severity scores*, and *psychotic score*.

Alcohol abstinence syndrome has a broad range of manifestations, each with a range of severities. Traditionally, alcohol withdrawal has been approached as a triad of three factors: hallucinations, tremor, and disorientation. Convulsions may be a part of the syndrome. The ASE Scale can be applied to alcohol abstinence syndrome as follows.

Factor 1 has been interpreted as the hallucinatory factor and includes sensory disturbances that contribute to hallucinogenesis such as nausea, vomiting, tinnitus, visual disturbances, paresthesias, muscle pain, pruritis, visual hallucinations, auditory hallucinations, tactile hallucinations, agitation, and sleep disturbances. Ostensibly, these signs and symptoms reflect the impact of withdrawal on the sensory systems and cortical sites.

Factor 2, the tremor factor, consists of tremor, sweating, depression, and anxiety. Evaluation does not presume that the anxiety and depression occur exclusively because of withdrawal, but that the withdrawal process may contribute to whatever anxiety and/or depression exists. The tremor factor presumably involves the impact of withdrawal on the autonomic nervous system.

Factor 3, the clouding of the sensorium factor, consists of altered states of consciousness, clouding of the sensorium, impaired contact, nystagmus, and disturbance of gait. These manifestations reflect brainstem functioning.

In using the ASE Scale in approximately 500 patients, we have found four following points to be useful in arriving at clinical decisions for treatment. First, the use of total score, selected severity score, and psychotic score is more meaningful than reliance on the three factors described above. Second, any patient with a total score of 10 or less and with a psychotic score of 0 can usually be managed in a supportive setting without the use of psychoactive medication. Third, the selected severity score appears to be an indicator of recovery from or progression in alcohol withdrawal syndrome. A rising selected severity score is an ominous sign; psychoactive medication is frequently indicated. Fourth, any patient with a psychotic score of >0 is a candidate for psychoactive medication.

It is possible to train paraprofessional personnel in the use of the ASE Scale; after establishing interrater reliability within a treatment system, the ASE Scale should provide the basis for making rational treatment decisions, eg, drug *v* nondrug treatment, medical *v* nonmedical setting.

Although alcohol withdrawal syndrome of the delirium tremens variety can progress in an unpredictable manner, numerous factors often contribute to increasing the severity of signs and symptoms:

• *The drinking pattern* — This includes the amount of alcohol consumed over a given period of time, ie, how rapidly the alcohol was consumed. The higher the BAC and the longer the BAC was maintained the more serious the withdrawal pattern will be. For example, a person who drinks a pint of whiskey in 60 minutes may experience a more serious abstinence syndrome than a person who consumed a fifth of whiskey over a 12-hour period.

• *The type of beverage alcohol* can also make a difference; consumption of those beverages with a high congener content can result in a more serious withdrawal.

• *The age of the patient*—severity of the syndrome increases with age.

• *Previous history of severe withdrawal symptoms*—If a patient has previously experienced advanced stages of withdrawal, eg, hallucinations, delusions, and seizures, there is a likelihood that the current abstinence syndrome will be more severe; the likelihood of seizures is also greater.

• *General physical condition*—Medical and/or surgical complications enhance the severity of the abstinence syndrome.

• *General psychological condition*—A marked disturbance in premorbid functioning, the coexistence of functional psychiatric disorders (including organic mental disorders) predisposes the patient to more severe and psychiatrically bizarre forms of abstinence syndrome.

Treatment Considerations and Rational Psychopharmacotherapy

Initially, in considering treatment of a patient who is withdrawing from alcohol, it must be decided whether psychoactive medication is even indicated. Many patients suffering stage I withdrawal or those who have a total ASE score (0 psychotic score) of 10 or less and who do not exhibit an increase in severity of symptoms require no medication. However, in some patients with more intense signs and symptoms, short-term use of psychoactive medication is indicated. Four guidelines for rational psychopharmacotherapy include:

First, know the pharmacology of the drug. Because of the phenomenon of cross-tolerance, the acutely withdrawing patient often requires higher dosages for adequate control. In addition, there are a number of drugs with potentially serious side effects that can exacerbate the pathophysiology of acute withdrawal. For instance, there are no specific advantages to using neuroleptics (major tranquilizers) in withdrawal states that do not include psychotic symptoms. The phenothiazines can reduce the seizure threshold as well as cause hypotension and cardiac arrhythmias.

Second, avoid oversedation. Because many patients can be managed on an ambulatory basis without hospitalization, amelioration of withdrawal signs and symptoms without iatrogenic somnolence is the desired therapeutic goal.

Third, avoid polypharmacy. If one psychotropic is ineffective in appropriate dosages, discontinue that particular drug and administer another rather than continue the medication.

Fourth, avoid secondary hyperarousal. If a benzodiazepine or other seda-
tive-hypnotic is chosen, gradual dosage reduction over a two to three-day
period is necessary to avoid the emergence of a rebound hyperarousal.

Although a number of claims have been made that one psychoactive agent
is clearly superior to all others, evidence to support such claims is equivocal.
It is important to become familiar with the use of only a small number of
agents and to individualize treatment with each patient.

If the use of a psychotropic appears warranted, we have found the following
approach to be useful in both inpatient and outpatient settings.

For stage I symptoms, hydroxyzine (Vistaril, Atarax) 50 to 100 mg either
intramuscularlarly IM or p.o. every 30 to 60 minutes as control offers the
advantages of sedation without a secondary hyperarousal upon abrupt discontinuation of the drug. Frequently, control can be achieved within a few hours,
and further drug administration is unnecessary. Hydroxyzine has no know
hepatotoxicity, no known cardiovascular toxicity except for anticholinergic
effects, and is relatively safe to administer to a patient with a blood alcohol
level who is also in serious withdrawal. It also has an antiemetic effect.

The disadvantages of hydroxyzine are that it lacks anticonvulsant effect and
cannot be given intravenously (IV). In addition, IM injection of hydroxyzine
is painful, and if it is not administered properly, a sterile abscess can result.

Hydroxyzine has almost no potential to produce physical dependency, making it particularly useful on an outpatient basis.

If hydroxyzine is ineffective or if the patient has a previous seizure history,
a benzodiazepine such as diazepam (Valium 10 to 20 mg IV or p.o. every 30
to 60 minutes) or chlordiazepoxide 50 to 100 mg p.o. or 25 to 50 mg IV every
30 to 60 minutes as control offers rapid and effective sedation, affords an
anticonvulsant effect and can be given IV in emergency situations (IV administration should be used only when resuscitation equipment is available).
Gradual dosage reduction is necessary to avoid rebound hyperarousal.

Use of phenobarbital 60 to 100 mg every 1 to 2 hours (IM, p.o., IV) as
necessary for control offers the advantages of significant anticonvulsant effect, a partially nonhepatic route of excretion (most patients in acute withdrawal have some liver damage), the option of IV administration, effective
sedation, and low cost.

As with the benzodiazepines, gradual dosage reduction is necessary to obviate rebound hyperarousal. A major disadvantage of phenobarbital is the
frequent requirement of rather large doses (eg, 300–600 mg) for control
because of cross-tolerance of the alcoholic to barbiturates. Because of a
relatively slow excretion rate, these large doses of phenobarbital can lead to
a generalized lethargy and obtundation, which can persist beyond the time
necessary for detoxication.

The physician is increasingly challenged with patients who are dually dependent on alcohol and other sedatives (ie, alcohol and Valium). We feel that phenobarbital is the drug of choice in treating the combined withdrawal states; frequent dosage adjustment is often necessary and the time required for total detoxication is of longer duration—often two to three weeks.

Thus, the management of combined alcohol and sedative withdrawal is similar to that for alcohol withdrawal alone, except that duration of psychopharmacotherapy is greater. In patients suffering polydrug dependence (ie, alcohol and/or sedatives and/or opioids and/or psychostimulants), the withdrawal phenomena should be clinically addressed, separately but simultaneously.

For stage II symptoms, haloperidol (Haldol) 5 mg IM every 3 to 4 hours p.r.n. produces effective hallucinolysis and can be used safely with an antihistamine (hydroxyzine) or a sedative (benzodiazepine, phenobarbital). Polypharmacy may be indicated. More than one or two doses of haloperidol are seldom required.

In management of stage III withdrawal syndrome, the most important considerations are the diagnosis and treatment of complicating medical–surgical conditions. Adequate sedation (often requiring high doses of hydroxyzine or a sedative) and use of haloperidol generally affords adequate control.

If the psychopharmacological management of the hyperarousal state of alcohol withdrawal were the only treatment necessary, management of this syndrome would indeed be simplified. However, alcohol has been termed "man's psychological blessing and physiological curse." Some pathophysiological disturbances that frequently coexist with and probably complicate and exacerbate alcohol withdrawal syndrome are amenable to diagnosis and treatment.

Although many physiological systems are affected by alcohol intoxication and withdrawal, attention should be paid to a few of the more serious disturbances in order to decrease the morbidity of withdrawal.

Although the diuretic effect of alcohol is well recognized, the total effect of alcohol on fluid and electrolyte balance should be appreciated.[11,12]

Alcohol exerts a diuretic effect by inhibiting the release of the antidiuretic hormone only when the blood alcohol level is rising; the extent of the diuresis correlates directly and proportionately with the rate of rise. With a decreasing BAC, there is actually an antidiuresis, caused by an increased release of the antidiuretic hormone and concomitant solute (primarily Na^+) retention by the kidneys (Figure 3.2).

The ultimate effect of repeated exposure to alcohol is an increase in total body water. Because of the associated solute retention, this fluid expansion is isosmotic in nature and is reflected in increases in both the extracellular and intracellular fluid spaces, including those of the brain. The urinary excretion of sodium and, to a lesser degree, potassium and chloride is reduced;

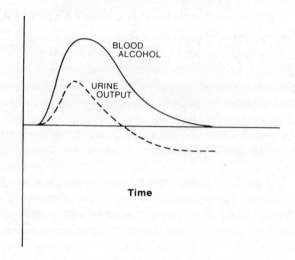

Figure 3.2. Relationship between blood alcohol and urine output.

in addition, Na^+ accumulates in the intracellular compartment, thus altering cell membrane potential (Figure 3.3). Conversely, alcohol causes a renal loss of magnesium (decreased magnesium reabsorption); hypomagnesemia is not an uncommon finding in alcohol abstinence syndrome. Although hypokalemia has been reported, this usually does not reflect a decrease in total exchangeable K^+ unless caused by protracted vomiting and/or diarrhea. More

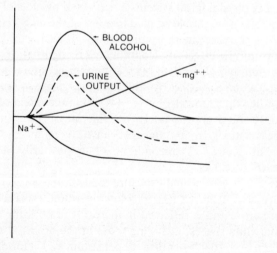

Figure 3.3. Relationship between blood alcohol, urine output, and solute excretion.

often, hypokalemia is a consequence of respiratory alkalosis with a shift of K^+ to the intracellular space in exchange for H^+, which moves to the extracellular space. In view of these fluid and electrolyte abnormalities, the following treatment guidelines are essential.

1. The regular, chronic excessive use of alcohol per se does not cause dehydration. The dry mouth frequently perceived by the acutely withdrawing patient is not necessarily indicative of a decreased intracellular or extracellular fluid volume. The dry mouth can be caused by exhaling alcohol and metabolic by-products, which can exert a dessicating effect on the mucous membranes of the mouth; by a direct decrease in salivary flow; or by an increase in the viscosity of saliva. Therefore, the empirical use of IV fluids is contraindicated since this only causes further fluid expansion.
2. If dehydration does complicate the withdrawal syndrome, it is a consequence of another cause of fluid loss such as vomiting, diarrhea, or severe malnutrition. Appropriate fluid replacement therapy is necessary for these patients.
3. If the state of hydration is not clinically obvious, a urine osmolality can be quite revealing in that osmolalities of 150 to 250 mOsm/kg H_2O are frequently found (hyposthenuria), which is not consistent with dehydration.
4. In the obviously overhydrated patient, one or two doses of a diuretic (preferably an effective natriuretic) within the initial 48 hours has proven to be effective and safe.
5. If the overhydrated patient remains untreated, eg, no IV fluids and no diuretic therapy, fluid and electrolyte balance return to normal within four days after abstinence from alcohol.
6. Replacement of Mg^{2+} (2 mL 50% $MgSo_4$ IM t.i.d. for two to three days) is often a useful adjunct.
7. Although the empirical use of phenytoin is controversial in acute withdrawal, experimental studies have suggested that 300 to 400 mg of Dilantin p.o. for four days may produce a salutary effect by decreasing the alcohol-induced increase in intracellular Na^+ levels. However, this Dilantin regimen *does not* necessarily protect the seizure-prone patient from suffering a withdrawal convulsion.

During periods of alcohol ingestion (acute and chronic), there is a tendency toward both metabolic and respiratory acidosis.[13] However, during alcohol withdrawal, alkalosis, primarily of respiratory origin, appears to dominate. In more severe cases of abstinence syndrome (eg, stage III) careful assessment of acid–base disturbances and the subsequent correction of these disturbances will contribute significantly to the reduction of morbidity.

Alcohol alters the absorption and metabolism of carbohydrates, lipids, and proteins. Regardless of the dietary intake, the nutritional consequences of excessive alcohol intake may well affect the course of abstinence syndrome. In this regard, the effect of alcohol on carbohydrate and vitamin metabolism is of particular and immediate importance.

Alcohol impairs gluconeogenesis and reduces hepatic glycogen stores; thus, the stress of alcohol withdrawal, which physiologically should lead to increased blood glucose concentrations, may in fact result in hypoglycemia and/or a rapid decrease in blood sugar because of the depleted hepatic glycogen stores. Immediate nutritional therapy directed at stabilizing the blood sugar is important.

Excessive alcohol intake also affects vitamin metabolism by decreasing gastrointestinal absorption of vitamins, decreasing storage of vitamins, and decreasing conversion to active forms. Acute (also chronic) alcohol-dependent persons suffer major deficiency of the vitamin thiamine. Initial IM administration of thiamine (50 to 100 mg) for two to three days followed by p.o. administration corrects this important deficiency. We have observed a number of cases of iatrogenic Wernicke's encephalopathy when increased carbohydrate intake was *not* accompanied by thiamine therapy in the treatment of acute alcohol abstinence syndrome. Multivitamin supplements are usually considered routine; there is no convincing evidence that megavitamin therapy offers any benefit to the acutely withdrawing patient. Because of the adverse effect alcohol has on folate metabolism (decreased intake and absorption, decreased hepatic storage, decreased conversion to tetrahydrofolic acid [THFA]) and in view of the high incidence of macrocytosis in alcohol-dependent persons, some clinicians give folic acid (0.5 mg to 1 mg) t.i.d., p.o. daily for several days. If possible, the initial diet should be low in fat and high in carbohydrate and protein.

Other significant pathophysiologic conditions include infection. The patient suffering acute alcohol abstinence syndrome is particularly prone to infection; among the more common infections are pneumonia (bacterial, aspiration), skin infections, urinary tract infections, meningitis, tuberculosis, peritonitis, septicemia, and septic arthritis. Alcohol causes an infectious diathesis, ie, decreased granulocyte numbers, impaired granulocyte function, decreased number and function of T lymphocytes, and a decrease in plasma bactericidal activity. The infection in an acute alcoholic can progress rapidly to malignant stages. When possible, cultures and sensitivities should be obtained; however, the early and aggressive use of antibiotics is frequently necessary before culture and sensitivity results are available.

The effects of alcohol on judgment and motor coordination frequently result in many forms of trauma, which commonly accompany and complicate alcohol abstinence syndrome. Head trauma is a well-known complication. Although the manifestations of basilar skull fractures or acute subdural hematomas are usually evident in the patient, a particularly troublesome and often unsuspected condition is a chronic subdural hematoma. If the patient's history reveals any head trauma in the past several days or even weeks, one should suspect the possibility of a chronic subdural hematoma. Often a deteriorating mental status is more diagnostic of this condition than is the neurological examination, which can remain relatively normal until advanced stages of this condition have been reached.

Fractures are common, with rib fractures being present more often. Esophagitis, gastritis, and pancreatitis are also frequent complications that mandate appropriate management.

Any medical–surgical complication can transform an otherwise uncomplicated alcohol abstinence syndrome into much more serious and often floridly psychotic conditions (stage III).

Total medical management of the patient is essential for a rapid and safe recovery.

Toxic Psychoses Associated with Alcohol Abstinence Syndrome

It is extremely important to recognize that some variants of alcohol abstinence syndrome are first seen as medical–psychiatric emergencies, yet can be a part of or only remotely resemble the classic stage I, II, or III picture described above. Alcohol abuse or dependence can frequently complicate underlying psychiatric conditions such as the schizophrenias, affective disorders, and the severely disturbed premorbid personalities, with resultant toxic psychotic states. Differential diagnosis between these and the classical alcohol abstinence syndrome of the delirium tremens variety is critical since the psychopharmacologic approach is different and, in many cases, the ultimate psychiatric disposition of the case is more discriminating. There are six important diagnostic points to consider in differentiating the classical alcohol abstinence syndrome of the delirium tremens variety from other alcohol-related toxic psychoses:

Extent or absence of psychomotor agitation and autonomic hyperactivity. In many toxic psychoses, the vital signs may be within normal limits, with little or no agitation.

Type and nature of the hallucinations. In the classical type of alcohol abstinence syndrome when hallucinations are present, they are usually mixed. In some of the toxic psychoses, the hallucinations may be *primarily* visual or auditory. Indeed, when one encounters a patient suffering *only* visual or *only* auditory hallucinations, one should at least suspect a more serious underlying psychiatric disorder.

State of the sensorium. To evaluate the state of the sensorium, one must determine if there is coexistent disorientation in one or more spheres. In some toxic psychoses, psychotic symptoms occur in a patient who is oriented in regard to time, place, person, and intent. On the other hand, the delusions (and often hallucinations) observed in the classical type of withdrawal are usually accompanied by some degree of disorientation.

Relationship between delusions and hallucinations. When hallucinations and delusions occur in classical abstinence syndrome (stage III), there is usually no relationship between the contents of the hallucinatory experience and the delusional system(s). In some toxic psychoses (particularly alcohol hallucinosis), the delusional system is totally or at least partially based on the precedent and accompanying hallucinations.

Extent of amnesia of the psychotic episode. Although total or partial amnesia is fairly characteristic of the hallucinations of stages II and III of classical alcohol abstinence syndrome, this phenomenon does not apply universally to other forms of toxic psychoses. If a patient relates a history of having suffered "DTs" in the past and can recount vividly the details of the psychotic symptoms, the obvious lack of any amnestic process should suggest the possibility of a concomitant psychiatric disorder.

Onset in regard to the drinking pattern. Psychotic symptoms associated with classical withdrawal usually occur within the first 72 to 96 hours after the cessation of alcohol ingestion. However, in some of the other types of toxic psychoses, symptom onset may occur as long as seven to ten days after the last drink.

Although many distinct variants of toxic psychoses associated with abstinence from alcohol have been described, there is frequently an overlapping of symptomatology. Although these toxic psychoses occur relatively infrequently, differential diagnosis from the classical abstinence picture is essential for proper management.

The toxic psychoses logically can be categorized as organic mental disorders (DSM-III) due to brain dysfunction caused by acute and/or chronic alcohol ingestion.

Alcohol Idiosyncratic Intoxication

Alcohol idiosyncratic intoxication (formerly termed "pathological intoxication) is a toxic psychosis that is actually associated with alcohol intoxication rather than with the abstinence syndrome. There is still considerable controversy concerning the actual existence of the acute psychiatric disorder known as alcohol idiosyncratic intoxication. The use of alcohol associated with this syndrome may well be incidental rather than causal. The DSM-III has diagnostically categorized this syndrome patterned after the classical description: a disorder of sudden onset following the consumption of minimal amounts of alcohol (insufficient to produce obvious intoxication in most people) characterized by disorientation, primarily visual (occasionally auditory) hallucinations, paranoid delusions, aggression, often violent behavior atypical of the person when not drinking, lasting from a few minutes to a day or more, followed by a prolonged sleep with subsequent amnesia of the details of the psychotic event.

Three basic theories have been offered to explain pathological intoxication.

Alcohol-induced seizures. Alcohol-induced seizures are similar to psychomotor epilepsy. Although there have been a few reports of alcohol-activated EEG abnormalities in suspected cases, the reproducibility of this procedure and the general lack of significant correlation between clinical behaviors and alcohol-induced EEG abnormalities casts some doubt on this theory.

Dissociative state (possibly hysterical psychosis). Many persons diagnosed as having "pathological intoxication" have a tendency to deal with aggressive impulses by avoidance and denial. In these persons, the episode of pathological intoxication is usually associated with periods of considerable psychosocial pressure; the dissociative state might well have occurred without the alcohol.

Malingering ("a culturally-fostered rationalization"). Medico-legal interest in pathological intoxication as a form of legal insanity has caused some observers to suspect that this syndrome represents malingering for obvious secondary gain.

In all probability, all three of these explanations may be applicable.

The clinician seldom encounters a patient during the psychotic episode; instead, law enforcement personnel are usually summoned because of the violent aggressive behavior. Partial sedation (Valium or phenobarbital, with the comcomitant use of Haldol [haloperidol]) may be useful during the psychosis. Because of the tendency of this syndrome to recur in the same individual, the foundation of long-term treatment is total abstinence from alcohol.

Alcohol Hallucinosis

This syndrome can occur as early as 48 hours after blood alcohol levels begin to decline; however, onset of symptoms may not appear until four to seven days after the last drink. Alcohol hallucinosis is characterized by vivid auditory (rarely accompanied by visual) hallucinations, delusions (which are often based on the hallucinatory experience), and appropriate affective response to the hallucinations. The sensorium is usually clear, the autonomic and psychomotor agitation are frequently absent. In addition, there is little or no amnesia of the psychotic episode. There have been numerous attempts to diagnose these individuals subsequently as schizophrenic; however, clinical evidence does not support this. Once the patient has recovered from the episode there is usually evidence of a rather severely disturbed premorbid personality. Treatment consists of neuroleptic medication (eg, Haldol [haloperidol]) for a brief period of time. Prolonged neuroleptization is usually unnecessary.

Alcohol Amnestic Syndrome

Alcohol amnestic syndrome is a disorder characterized by impairment of short-term memory (inability to learn new information) and long-term memory (inability to remember past information) and is generally associated with prolonged, chronic heavy alcohol use and with vitamin (thiamine) deficiency. Alcohol amnestic syndrome due to thiamine deficiency has previously been termed Korsakoff's syndrome. Amnestic syndrome frequently follows an acute episode of Wernicke's encephalopathy. In addition to amnesia, other features include confabulation, disorientation (usually continuous), peripheral neuropathy (50% of the cases), and psychomotor agitation. This syndrome usually persists indefinitely, and only minimal improvement can be expected. The treatment approach includes a nutritious diet, vitamin supplements (particularly B_1 thiamine and B_6 pyridoxine), and care in a nonstressful environment. We have seen a few patients who appeared to show more than expected improvement with the addition of low doses of haloperidol (0.5 mg b.i.d.).

Alcohol Paranoid State

Alcohol paranoid state occurs almost exclusively in men >50 years of age, with severely disturbed premorbid functioning. It is preceded by many years of chronic excessive alcohol use. Characteristics of this toxic psychosis include excessive suspiciousness, distrust and jealousy, delusions of infidelity (particularly marital infidelity), latent homosexual feelings and fears, inappropriately violent behaviors (assaultive, homicidal), followed by amnesia of the psychotic episode. Although onset can occur within 48 to 72 hours after the last drink, it is not unusual for this to occur days later; this syndrome can be intermittent and can last for days to weeks even if the patient is abstinent. Hospitalization is necessary because of the potential for violence. Patients respond rapidly to neuroleptic medication (eg, Haldol); however, it may be necessary to continue neuroleptic medication for weeks or even months.

Dementia Associated with Alcohol Dependence

After many years of heavy alcohol use (alcohol dependence) some individuals develop a rather gradual and insidious onset of a marked impairment of cognition accompanied by some memory loss, interference with vocational and/or social functioning due to a decrease in intellectual abilities, impairment in abstract thinking and judgment, and other disturbances of higher cortical functions such as aphasia, apraxia, and agnosia. Diagnosis is based on persistence of the dementia for at least three weeks after cessation of alcohol use. Some improvement can be expected with a nutritious diet, vitamin supplement, and abstinence from alcohol; however, prognosis is generally poor, and satisfactory levels of social and occupational functioning are seldom attained.

Finally, if the patient suffering the acute phase of alcohol dependence can be managed in surroundings in which staff–patient interaction is nonjudgmental and nonmoralistic, the benefit of tender loving care (TLC) is obvious. Emergency medical and nonmedical services should be prepared to diagnose the variants of the acute phase of alcohol dependence and to provide or arrange for the provision of appropriate medical–psychiatric intervention. Treating the acute alcoholic is perhaps the easiest task; if treatment is accomplished in a skillful and well-informed manner, the patient is often much more amenable to entering a longer-term treatment program, so vital for a favorable prognosis.

REFERENCES

1. Chafetz MD: Foreward, in Pavlov CG (ed): *Proceedings: Alcoholic Emergency Care Services*. National Institute of Alcohol Abuse and Alcoholism, DHEW publication (HSM), 73-9024. Government Printing Office 1972.
2. Whitfield CL, Thompson G, Lamb A, et al: Detoxification of 1024 alcoholic patients without psychoactive drugs. *JAMA* 239:1409–1410, 1978.
3. Den Hartog GL: A decade of detox: Development of non-hospital approaches to alcohol detoxification – A review of the literature. Substance Abuse Monograph Series, State of Missouri Division of Alcohol and Drug Abuse 1982, No. 2-82, 1967.
4. Knott DH, Fink RD: Problems surrounding emergency care services for acute alcoholism. *Hosp Community Psychiatry* 26:42–43, 1975.
5. Knott DH, Fink RD, Morgan JC: Intoxication and the alcohol abstinence syndrome, in Schwartz GR, Sofar P, Stone JH, et al (eds): *Principles and Practice of Emergency Medicine*. Philadelphia, Saunders, 1978, pp 1345–1350.
6. Sellers EM, Kalant K: Alcohol intoxication and withdrawal. *N Engl J Med* 294:757–762, 1976.
7. Feldman DJ, Pattison EM, Sobell LC: Outpatient alcohol detoxification: Initial findings on 564 patients. *Am J Psychiatry* 132:407–412, 1975.
8. Beard JD, Knott DH, Fink RD: The use of plasma and urine osmolality in evaluating the acute phase of alcohol abuse. *South Med J* 67:271–273, 1974.
9. Gitlow SE: An overview in alcoholism, in Gitlow SE, Peyser HS (eds): *Alcoholism: A Practical Treatment Guide*. Orlando, Fla, Grune & Stratton, 1980, pp 1–22.
10. Knott DH, Lerner WD, Fink RD, et al: Decision for alcohol detoxication: A method to standardize patient evaluation. *Postgrad Med* 69:65–78, 1981.
11. Beard JD, Knott DH: Fluid and electrolyte balance during acute withdrawal in chronic alcoholic patients. *JAMA* 204:135–139, 1968.
12. Knott DH, Beard JD: A diuretic approach to acute withdrawal from alcohol. *South Med J* 62:485–489, 1969.
13. Sargent WQ, Beard JD, Knott DH: Acid base following ethanol intake and during acute withdrawal from ethanol, in Majchrowicz E, Noble E (eds): *Biochemistry and Pharmacology of Ethanol*, vol 2. New York, Plenum, 1979, pp 17–25.

Chapter 4
ALCOHOL DEPENDENCE: SUBACUTE PHASE

The subacute phase of alcohol dependence is a condition involving medi-cal–psychiatric, psychological and social problems directly or indirectly con-sequential to a person's use of alcohol. Frequently, overt signs of alcohol dependence are not obvious.

Persons suffering the subacute phase of alcohol dependence frequent physi-cians' offices and hospitals with myriad illnesses that may be caused by, com-plicated by, or exacerbated by the regular use of alcohol. This subacute phase has two clinical implications for practicing physicians.

First, after being detoxified from acute alcohol abstinence syndrome, the patient has certain persisting medical and psychiatric problems that require the diagnostic acumen and treatment skill of a physician.

Second, the same medical–psychiatric problems associated with alcohol use occur more frequently in persons who are not grossly intoxicated, do not suf-fer abstinence syndrome, and in whom the diagnosis of alcohol dependence may not be immediately apparent.

Individuals suffering the subacute phase are consistently frequent recipients of health care. It is estimated that 18% to 25% of all patients who are medical–surgical admissions to a general hospital suffer disorders related to alcohol use; 25% to 35% of all psychiatric patient admissions (inpatient and outpatient) have diagnoses that are alcohol-related or are complicated by alcohol use. The unsuspected role played by alcohol in physiological and/or psychological health impairment often contributes to apparent treatment refractoriness and a high degree of recidivism.

The physician has a unique opportunity to practice preventive medicine at the secondary level by: (a) understanding the toxicity of alcohol in relation-ship to a number of common medical and psychological problems; (b) increas-ing the index of suspicion of alcohol's involvement in these problems; (c) tak-ing a thorough alcohol (and drug) history; (d) being observant for suggestive signs of excessive drinking on the physical examination and the mental status examination; and (e) appropriately interpreting laboratory parameters that are often altered by alcohol use.

The psychophysiologic problems of alcohol use frequently cause the individual to seek medical care. Some of the more common problems in the subacute phase involve metabolic abnormalities, impairment of physiologic systems, and psychological dysfunction. The above manifestations of ill health are commonly encountered in the general practice of medicine; recognition of the role exerted by alcohol use is tantamount to quality health care.

DIAGNOSTIC AND TREATMENT IMPLICATIONS OF METABOLIC ABNORMALITIES

Fluid and Electrolyte Metabolism

The chronic, prodigious use of alcohol results in overhydration with Na^+ retention, which increases morbidity of alcohol abstinence syndrome. However, the altered fluid and electrolyte balance can exist in the absence of clinically significant withdrawal phenomena and is frequently manifest as protracted, recurrent, or refractory edema, a common complaint and sign in clinical practice.[1] Excessive alcohol consumption can result in chronic overhydration; one must suspect that the patient with recurrent or refractory edema of otherwise unknown etiology may be alcohol dependent. In addition, whenever a patient with edema from any cause is treated (eg, diuretic, fluid restriction, etc), the admonition to abstain completely from alcohol during the treatment period is an integral part of the overall regimen.

Carbohydrate Metabolism

Two commonly encountered clinical entities in medicine are carbohydrate intolerance and hypoglycemia, both of which can result directly from the excessive use of alcohol.[2]

Severe hypoglycemia associated with an acute alcohol debauch has been documented primarily in patients with increased susceptibility to the hypoglycemic effects of ethanol, such as infants, children, adolescents, the elderly, and those individuals with poor nutrition. However, hypoglycemia can be observed in patients who are not overtly malnourished.

Chronic alcohol use impairs gluconeogenesis, which results in depleted glycogen stores. Thus, in times of stress, the capacity for desired glycogenolytic response to increased blood sugar is impaired. Symptoms of hypoglycemia frequently occur in the late afternoon. Characteristics of a typical person with hypoglycemia consequent to the chronic excessive use of alcohol are:

- Poor dietary habits—five to six cups of coffee per day, heavy smoking, omission of breakfast and, frequently, of lunch
- Daytime use of alcohol—the "martini for lunch bunch"
- Type A personality traits
- Consumption of primarily distilled spirits—as opposed to beer and wine
- Complaints of easy fatigability, late afternoon "jitters" including decreased frustration tolerance, hyperirritability
- Glucose tolerance test results—FBS normal, blood sugars at 1, 2, and 3 hours after standard glucose load of 120, 80, and 40, respectively, with concomitant symptoms of hypoglycemia

Although there are many causes of hypoglycemia, when this condition is detected with routine examinations or when it is suspected by history and subsequently validated, the physician should suspect excessive alcohol use. Treatment consists of a diet that is high in protein and moderate to low in carbohydrates, abstinence from alcohol, caffeine, and nicotine, and, in some cases, psychotherapy.

The association between glucose intolerance and frank diabetes mellitus in those patients with liver disease secondary to alcohol dependence (45% to 70%) has long been recognized. However, there are a number of heavy drinkers who have no discernible liver disease but who exhibit carbohydrate intolerance. Frequently, these individuals are labeled as having "early" or "latent" diabetes mellitus and are treated accordingly when the etiologic role of alcohol use is not suspected. If such patients are placed on a diabetic diet and are further given hypoglycemic agents but continue to consume alcohol, acute and chronic hypoglycemia can occur.

The typical patient without liver disease who presents with glucose intolerance secondary to alcohol use usually has the following characteristics: (a) age 40 years or older, often with a family history of adult onset diabetes; poor dietary habits but not overtly malnourished; (c) history of excessive alcohol use for five years or longer; and (d) glucose tolerance test results of FBS high normal, 1-, 2-, 3-hour blood sugars after a standard glucose load of 200, 190, and 180 respectively.

It is easy to assume that a diabetic process is operational based on these data; however, in many cases, the diagnosis of diabetes mellitus is unwarranted, and treatment of the alcohol dependence results in the return of carbohydrate metabolism to normal.

The cause(s) of the alcohol-induced carbohydrate intolerance is presently speculative. Some theories are that there is peripheral resistance to endogenous insulin, that occult subclinical chronic pancreatitis exists, or that the patient has hepatic metabolic dysfunction not detectable with the commonly used liver function tests.

The differential diagnosis of "diabetes mellitus" in any adult patient should include the possibility of alcohol-induced carbohydrate intolerance. In fact, it is difficult to offer a valid interpretation of the glucose tolerance test in *any* patient who has not been alcohol-free for at least two weeks. Care must be taken not to overdiagnose diabetes mellitus in the heavy drinker and thereby avoid dealing directly with the alcohol problem. Furthermore, use of alcohol should be discouraged in all patients who suffer from diabetes mellitus.

Treatment of alcohol-induced carbohydrate intolerance includes abstinence from alcohol and adequate nutrition through improved dietary habits.

Uric Acid Metabolism

The association between gout and heavy alcohol use has long been recognized. Unfortunately, "gout" is frequently overdiagnosed in an alcohol-dependent patient based on elevated serum uric acid levels with no clear-cut signs and symptoms of gout. Alcohol use increases serum lactic acid in anyone who drinks. The elevated lactic acid competes with uric acid for renal secretion, with the result that renal secretion of uric acid is impaired. Thus, the increased serum uric acid associated with alcohol use is due to decreased elimination rather than increased production. Asymptomatic hyperuricemia often results from chronic, heavy use of alcohol. In these cases, the diagnosis of gout is not warranted, and uricosuric agents should be avoided. Abstinence from alcohol or a marked change in drinking pattern generally results in normal uric acid levels.

Lipid Metabolism

It is now well established that both acute and chronic alcohol consumption can produce rather dramatic elevations in plasma lipid concentrations.[3] Because many individuals who consume excessive amounts of alcohol on a chronic basis have normal lipid levels, there must be an underlying heterogeneity in the drinking population.

Triglyceride levels are affected most profoundly, but changes can also be observed in cholesterol, phospholipids, and free fatty acids. The hyperlipemic response to alcohol appears to be related to the magnitude, duration, and chronicity of the blood alcohol concentration, with some adaptation occurring with time. This hyperlipemic response is exacerbated by the concomitant ingestion of alcohol and dietary fat.

Electrophoretic pattern of alcohol-induced hyperlipidemia indicates an increase in very-low-density lipoprotein (VLDL) and chylomicrons. The most prevalent pattern is a type 4 Frederickson classification, with a primary increase in VLDL and a dense staining pre-beta band. A second, less frequent pattern is a Frederickson type 5, with elevations in both VLDL and chylo-microns. These patterns can occur in heavy drinkers who do not have familial or primary hyperlipidemia; however, in those individuals with familial hyper-lipidemia, the alcohol-induced hyperlipemic effect is greater.

The epidemiological and clinical significance of hyperlipidemia associated with alcohol use is still open to question and debate. It is apparent, however, that the risk of pancreatitis in the heavy chronic drinker is significantly higher if hyperlipidemia is present.

High-density lipoprotein (HDL) is also increased with alcohol use. The alleged protective effect of increased HDL on the atherosclerotic process has been used to explain the apparent reduced incidence of atherosclerosis in the clearly identified alcoholic. This assumption is still controversial; in fact, some clinicians use elevated HDL (>60) as a biochemical parameter suggesting heavy drinking and alcohol dependence, since alcohol-induced increases in HDL appear to be dose dependent.

If hyperlipidemia associated with heavy alcohol use exists, the physician should make an attempt to establish the presence or absence of familial hyperlipidemia in alcohol users who present with elevated lipids. Alcohol use in individuals with the familial pattern of hyperlipidemia may enhance the development of disorders such as pancreatitis and atherosclerosis. In addi-tion, the physician should advise all hyperlipidemic persons to abstain from alcohol for several weeks before being reevaluated. The individual who does not stop drinking may well have a serious drinking problem. Therefore, treat-ment considerations involve: (a) treatment of alcohol dependence, if it is etiological or a complicating factor in the hyperlipidemia (abstinence is fre-quently curative); (b) diet management; and (c) possible use of nicotinic acid (3 to 4.5 gm/day). Effectiveness of drug therapy in an alcohol-dependent population is not well documented, however.

Vitamin Metabolism

Persons who chronically consume large doses of alcohol often state: "I can drink all I want so long as I take my vitamins and eat well." As a result of such a theory being put into practice, alcohol abuse and alcohol dependence represent the single leading cause of vitamin deficiency in this country.[4]

Primary vitamin deficiencies can result from inadequate dietary intake (limited or sporadic), which is frequently associated with alcohol use. The primary type occurs more often in an obviously malnourished indigent alco-holic population and is manifest with overt clinical signs of vitamin deficiency. However, secondary deficiencies are much more common and result from the direct and indirect effect of alcohol use on vitamin metabolism. This second-ary type is often covert and subclinical in regard to signs and symptoms and becomes significant only when a superimposed metabolic stress transpires. The apparent causes of the alcohol-induced secondary vitamin deficiences include decreased absorption, decreased storage, ineffective utilization, decreased conversion to metabolically active forms, or a combination of these factors.

Although various studies suggest an alcohol-induced adverse impact on all of the known vitamins, clinically significant conditions appear to involve a few major vitamins.

Thiamine

Thiamine appears to be the vitamin most profoundly affected by alcohol. In healthy, nonalcohol-dependent subjects, ethanol can impair thiamine absorption; in persons who abuse or who are dependent on alcohol, this effect is augmented. It may require two to three months of abstinence from alcohol and an adequate diet before thiamine metabolism returns to normal. The initial dose of thiamine (100 mg) replacement should be given IM; thiamine administration (100 mg daily p.o.) for three months may also be efficacious. Concomitant magnesium depletion appears to escalate the neurological sequelae of thiamine deficiency since there is a relationship between magnesium and thiamine in regard to a specific thiamine-dependent enzyme. Concomitant acute or chronic liver injury also interferes with the utilization of thiamine.

Folic Acid

A functional folate deficiency results in heavy drinkers in the presence or absence of liver disease and represents an alcohol-induced impairment of folic acid absorption and impaired intracellular utilization of folate. Folic acid deficiency can exist even with normal serum folic acid levels and is frequently manifested biochemically as an increase in the mean corpuscular volume (MCV) of the erythrocyte. There appears to be a solid rationale for treating alcohol abusers and alcohol-dependent individuals with doses of folic acid in excess of the minimum daily requirements, eg, 5 mg folic acid daily for two to three months.

Vitamin B_6 (pyridoxine)

A deficiency of Vitamin B_6 has been described in chronic alcoholic subjects consequent to alcohol-induced hepatic injury and an increased urinary excretion of this vitamin. Studies suggest that pyridoxine replacement facilitates tissue regeneration after cellular (especially hepatic) injury.

Vitamin B$_{12}$

The adverse effect of alcohol on gastric function, eg, decreased availability of the intrinsic factor and the change in the absorption capacity of the small intestine, tends to produce a Vitamin B$_{12}$ deficiency. Many persons believe that the macrocytosis of the erythrocyte seen frequently in alcohol-dependent patients results from a combined folate–Vitamin B$_{12}$ deficiency. Replacement of Vitamin B$_{12}$ may expedite recovery from tissue injury.

Vitamins A, D, and K

Alcohol-dependent persons with chronic liver disease have a malabsorption of Vitamins A, D, and K, which leads to steatorrhea. There is no evidence that megavitamin therapy is superior to the regular use of vitamins in slightly larger doses than the minimum daily requirement. During the initial three months of nutritional treatment, a reasonable regimen might include thiamine 100 mg p.o. daily for three months; folic acid 5 mg p.o. daily or b.i.d. for three months; and a multivitamin b.i.d. for three months.

The effect of vitamin therapy is significantly mitigated if alcohol use continues. Further, daily vitamin therapy does not necessarily preclude the development of certain vitamin-deficient states with the heavy daily use of alcohol.

DIAGNOSTIC AND TREATMENT IMPLICATIONS OF IMPAIRMENT OF PHYSIOLOGICAL SYSTEMS

Central Nervous System (CNS)

Historically, it has been recognized that "chronic alcoholism" is associated with a deterioration of CNS function.[5] Attention focused on neuropathological changes has yielded excellent descriptions of the Wernicke-Korsakoff psychosis, a focal cerebellar syndrome, degeneration of the corpus callosum, central pontine myelinosis, the sequelae of trauma associated with alcohol intoxication, and cerebral atrophy disparate for the age of the subject. Postulated etiological factors for these syndromes include direct neurotoxicity of alcohol and/or its metabolic by-products, associated malnutrition, trauma, and generalized metabolic abnormalities. Indeed, the cognitive and behavioral changes noted in chronic alcoholics have been likened to an "accelerated aging process."

Recently, with the more generalized use and interpretation of neuropsychological tests, a much more subtle and covert impairment of CNS function has been described in alcohol-dependent patients with regard to subclinical brain damage. This form of brain dysfunction is often manifest as consummate denial of drinking problems and apparent resistance to treatment efforts, often interpreted by the physician to mean that such patients really do not want help. Although intellectual functioning does not appear to be significantly impaired after detoxification, there can be demonstrable defects in sensory-motor performance, perceptual capacities, conceptual shifting, visual-spatial abstracting abilities, and memory; all of these elements can certainly impair the overall adaptive abilities of alcohol-abusing and alcohol-dependent persons. It has been estimated that from 50% to 70% of detoxified alcohol-dependent persons entering treatment suffer from subclinical dysfunction as described above. The impact on treatment modalities and treatment outcome expectations is obvious. Early assessment and diagnosis of neuropsychological deficits such as memory loss, decreased attention span, and cognitive dysfunctions is essential in formulating a realistic treatment approach. This can be easily accomplished by a modified mental status examination, which will be discussed later. Vitamin therapy, adequate nutrition, and abstinence from alcohol are the cornerstones of medical therapy; sedatives are generally contraindicated.

Peripheral Nervous System

The direct neurotoxic effects of alcohol, in addition to nutritional deficiences, cause axonal degeneration in both the sensory and motor portions of the peripheral nervous system.[5] The clinical signs and symptoms include pain, hypesthesia, paresthesia, and diminished vibratory sense, initially involving the distal portion of the lower extremities, but in later stages affecting the upper extremities as well. These neuropathic changes are usually accompanied by muscle weakness. It is estimated that 10% of hospitalized alcohol-dependent persons exhibit this clinical syndrome; however, recent evidence suggests that 70% to 75% of alcohol-dependent patients may suffer subclinical forms of peripheral nerve damage. Abstinence from alcohol and vitamin and nutritional therapy usually lead to marked improvement over a relatively prolonged period of time (three to nine months).

Respiratory System

Acute and chronic intoxication impairs several protective aspects of respiratory function, which results in a much higher incidence of pulmonary pathology in alcohol-dependent v non–alcohol-dependent persons.[6] These protective mechanisms include: the cough reflex, since alcohol depresses normal reflex of glottis closure; mucociliary function, since alcohol causes dehydration of the mucous layer and markedly decreases and even stops ciliary movement; and phagocytosis and destruction of material by alveolar macrophages, since alcohol selectively inhibits alveolar macrophage functioning.

Basic and clinical research data suggest that alcohol-induced impairment

of these mechanisms causes an increased incidence of infection and parenchymal destruction. Heavy smoking, common in alcoholics, is not solely
responsible for these changes.

Infections

Pneumococcal pneumonia is the most common form of pneumonia found
in alcohol-dependent persons; morbidity and mortality are augmented by
acute and chronic alcohol use. There is also a higher frequency of Gram-
negative infections, with *Klebsiella pneumoniae* being the most frequent
organism, followed by *Enterobacteriaceae, E. coli*, and *Pseudomonas*. Because of a generalized dysfunction of the immmune mechanism (vide infra),
the pneumoniae in alcoholics are rapidly progressive. There is often a leuko-
penic rather than a leukocytic response to pulmonary infections.

Aspiration pneumonia (mainly food material and gastric juices) causes a
severe explosive and widely distributed process requiring immediate attention
(antibiotic and corticosteroid therapy). Approximately 70% of all lung ab-
scesses are found in the alcohol-dependent population. The pathogens are
varied; poor dental hygiene appears to be a significant predisposing factor
in addition to depression of the cough reflex.

Although detection, prophylaxis, and treatment of pulmonary tuberculosis
have caused a remarkable decrease in this disorder, alcoholics as a group have
a higher incidence of this disease than do groups suffering other types of
chronic diseases. Because of a higher degree of noncompliance with treatment,
alcoholics with tuberculosis not only have a poor prognosis, but are foci for
the spread of this disease and for the emergence of resistant organisms.

Emphysema, fibrosis, and bronchiectasis, which occur more frequently in
an alcoholic *v* nonalcoholic population, result not only from repeated infections, but also from the direct effect of alcohol on pulmonary parenchyma.
It has been postulated, based on experimental evidence, that alcohol and its
metabolites, in addition to causing dehydration of the mucous layer of the
tracheobronchial tree, cause direct parenchymal damage by denaturing proteins.

When the physician is faced with a patient who has recurrent and/or refractory pulmonary problems such as bronchitis, pneumonia, and exacerbation
of various forms of chronic lung disease, alcohol abuse and dependence
should certainly be suspected. Failure to recognize and treat the alcohol problem will yield poor results in treatment of the respiratory tract problem.

Cardiovascular System

The deleterious effects of acute and chronic alcohol ingestion on the heart
and blood vessels have long been recognized; however, research interest in
and clinical appreciation of this area have only recently begun to flourish.[7,8]

Early reports which suggested that alcohol was directly cardiotoxic were offset by the assumption that nutritional and vitamin deficiencies associated with heavy alcohol use were necessary ingredients to the production of cardiovascular disease. The societal ambivalence toward the benefit-risk ratio of alcohol consumption was reflected in the endorsement of alcohol use in various cardiovascular disorders such as angina pectoris, hypertension, and obliterative vascular disease. During the past decade, this concept has not been widely accepted by clinicians; however, recent suggestions that alcohol might exert a "protective effect" in the development of coronary atherosclerosis is again causing confusion and controversy.

Circulatory Disease: Morbidity and Mortality

The disease concept of alcoholism has prompted a number of mortality and morbidity studies of alcoholics and heavy drinking populations. The mortality in these populations exceeded the expected death rate, and cardiovascular mortality constituted 20% of the excess.

Although morbidity data are not extensive, studies do suggest that vocational dysfunction secondary to cardiovascular diseases was 1.9 times greater in an employed population v matched controls.

There is no reason to doubt the direct toxic effects of alcohol on the cardiovascular system; however, other factors such as heavy smoking, nutritional and metabolic abnormalities, and life-style certainly contribute to the enhanced circulatory disease mortality and morbidity in heavy-drinking and alcohol-dependent persons.

Heavy smoking: Most heavy drinkers are also heavy smokers; epidemiologically, cigarette smoking has been established as a major risk factor for ischemic heart disease and hypertension. Whether or not heavy smoking and heavy drinking act in concert additively or synergistically is not known. Studies reveal that the consumption of three or more drinks per day results in higher systolic and diastolic pressures in both men and women, independent of smoking, and hypertension is known to play a role in circulatory disease mortality and morbidity.

Nutritional-metabolic abnormalities: The chronic and prodigious use of alcohol adversely affects nutrition and metabolism, and can have negative impact on normal cardiovascular functioning. Among these effects are hyperlipidemia; vitamin deficiencies, especially thiamine and vitamin C; protein deficiency; carbohydrate intolerance; hypoglycemia; and abnormalities in mineral metabolism, with reduction in total exchangeable magnesium, Na^+ retention and increase in intracellular Na^+ in the myocardium (and possibly the intima of the peripheral vasculature), alterations in Ca^{2+} metabolism, and deficiencies in and abnormal metabolism of zinc.

Life-style patterns of alcoholics, such as neglect of health, physical inactivity, and lack of compliance with prevention and treatment regimens, may contribute to alcohol-related circulatory disease mortality and morbidity.

These factors, coupled with the direct cardiovascular toxicity of alcohol, mandate a continuing search for mechanisms and processes, since cardiovascular disease per se leads all other causes of morbidity and mortality in this and many other countries.

Physiological Considerations

Cardiac Metabolism. The acute administration of ethanol to experimental animals and chronic alcoholic subjects results in an immediate increase in myocardial triglyceride content. The initial response is an increase in triglyceride uptake by the heart in the absence of triglyceridemia. Secondarily, there appears to be an enhanced triglyceride production by cardiac tissue, utilizing as a substrate increased available amounts of acetate consequent to alcohol metabolism. Studies which focus on the chronic experimental administration of alcohol reveal that the glyceride content remains elevated but will return to normal following the patient's abstinence from alcohol. Accompanying the increase in myocardial triglyceride uptake and production, there is a concomitant decrease in free fatty acid uptake by the heart. With these changes in lipid metabolism, there is an increase in cardiac uptake of glucose, lactate, and acetate, the metabolism of which temporarily impairs the primary utilization of lipids for energy. It appears that both the acute and chronic ingestion of alcohol changes the formation and utilization of substrates, resulting in less efficient energy production.

Although there is a major effect on cardiac lipids, alcohol also exerts a profound effect on mineral metabolism. Potassium and phosphate egress from cardiac tissue occurs after an acute insult with alcohol and is similar to that seen in ischemic necrosis; it appears to be rapidly reversible, however. Acute and chronic alcohol ingestion in the experimental situation (canine) leads to an increase in intracellular Na^+ content, which is reversible with abstinence from alcohol. Recent advances in knowledge of excitation–contraction coupling mechanisms and the effect that acute and chronic alcohol consumption exerts in this regard are pertinent to the impact that ethanol has on cardiac performance. Although direct alcohol-induced mitochondrial damage leads to metabolic defects, injury to the excitation–contraction coupling mechanism and contractile proteins occurs as well. Excitation–contraction coupling and relaxation in the myocardium results from interactions between the myofibrillar proteins actin and myosin and an energy-dependent calcium movement. The functional anatomic site for this process is the sarcoplasmic reticulum, which is damaged both structurally and biochemically by alcohol. In addition, the direct and indirect impairment of ATPase by alcohol may adversely affect the active uptake and transport of Ca^{2+}.

Chronic alcohol use leads to a deficiency in myocardial protein synthesis, obviously affecting the contractile elements. The effect on protein synthesis may be caused by acetaldehyde rather than ethanol per se.

The observation of zinc deficiencies, which can be caused by experimental chronic alcohol use and are involved with cardiac dysfunction, is stimulating further investigation into the role that alcohol-induced abnormalities in trace metal metabolism play in cardiac disease associated with alcoholism.

Cardiac Morphology. Alcohol-induced metabolic changes are generally thought to precede structural alterations. Based on the above discussion, one would expect these alterations to involve primarily mitochondria, sarcoplasmic reticulum, and contractile elements. The developmental progression of alcohol-induced morphological abnormalities in the heart appears to be as follows: mitochondrial swelling→increased mitochondrial lipid inclusions→degenerating mitochondrial cristae→intramuscular accumulation of lipids→swelling and degeneration of the sarcoplasmic reticulum→changes in the myocytes, with loss of cross-striation, pyknotic nuclei, vacuolization, and hydropic, fatty, and hyaline degeneration→areas of degeneration, fibrosis, and endocardial thickening. Coronary vessels show little evidence of arteriosclerotic change. These pathological findings have been described in experimental and clinical situations involving alcoholic cardiomyopathy and are extremely similar to the picture seen in cases of cardiomyopathy from other causes. The metabolic and structural aberrations are consonant with the effect of alcohol on cardiac function.

Cardiac Function. A number of experimental and clinical observations have suggested that alcohol causes a functional impairment of the heart even in the absence of clinical cardiac disease. Acute and chronic studies using invasive and noninvasive techniques and involving isolated cardiac muscle fibers, anesthetized and unanesthetized experimental animals, alcoholic patients with and without heart disease, and normal healthy subjects generally indicate that alcohol is a myocardial depressant that reduces contractility. This depressant activity is more pronounced if clinical heart disease (especially coronary artery disease) is coexistent.

Relatively little attention has been paid to the effect of alcohol on reflex activity of the cardiovascular system. A study involving healthy normal volunteers who ingested doses of alcohol characterized as "social drinking" indicated that acceleration of heart rate and peripheral vasoconstriction in response to stress were more pronounced in such consumption than in the absence of alcohol and suggested that alcohol enhances cardiovascular reflex modulation. Although this may be of little import in nonalcoholic physiologically healthy subjects, it may be significant in persons with underlying cardiac disease.

The metabolic and structural effects of alcohol on the contractile tissue of the heart appear in the conducting system also; thus, one would expect some electrophysiological consequences. Although there are a number of clinical reports describing EKG changes associated with "alcoholic" heart disease, there is little experimental evidence derived from either in vitro or in vivo studies of the effect of alcohol on the cardiac conducting system. Extensive investigation of the influence exerted by alcohol on skeletal muscle suggests that acute exposure to ethanol results in an increase in membrane conductance, lowering of membrane resistance, and a decrease in resting membrane potential, all of which appear to be dose-dependent. An increase in intracellular Na^+ in addition to alterations in the availability and binding of Mg^{2+} and Ca^{2+} may be implicated. The overall result appears to be a heightened excitability along with an increase in conduction time, as reflected by a prolongation of both depolarization and repolarization intervals. The depression by alcohol of the cardiac conduction system is augmented in patients with organic heart disease.

The inconsistency and controversy involving the effect of acute and chronic alcohol exposure in animal (and a few human) studies result from varying investigative approaches, eg, open-chest v closed-chest, anesthetized v unanesthetized animals, and the measurement of total coronary blood flow v regional cardiac blood flow. Because alcohol has been prescribed as a coronary vasodilator, further research is needed in this area. Even though studies have shown *an increase, a decrease,* or *no change* in coronary flow during the acute administration of alcohol, there is consensus that concomitant hemodynamic and metabolic consequences such as increased O_2 requirements, tachycardia, elevated systolic and diastolic blood pressure, and increased left ventricular end diastolic pressure offer cardiac benefits neither to persons with organic heart disease nor (probably) to normal healthy individuals.

Effect of Alcohol on the Central Circulation: Pathophysiological Considerations

Alcoholic Cardiomyopathy. Primary myocardial disease (PMD) that is not clearly secondary to congenital, hypertensive, or arteriosclerotic causes is attracting increasing etiologic, diagnostic, therapeutic, and prognostic consideration. The association between chronic heavy alcohol use and heart failure has been recognized for well over 100 years. Most clinicians now agree that although the combination of alcoholism and malnutrition are mutually exacerbating factors in the development of certain cases of PMD, alcohol itself can effect a cardiomyopathy.

The light and electron microscopic morphological abnormalities of alcoholic cardiomyopathy are generally indistinguishable from those associated with cardiomyopathies from other causes. An attractive postulate as to the pathogenesis of alcoholic heart disease involves pathology in the intramyocardial coronary arteries. A study that included a relatively young group of patients suffering from a "chronic alcoholic state" in whom there was no clinical evidence of alcoholic cardiomyopathy or of pathology of the large coronary arteries revealed four basic vascular abnormalities in the intramyocardial small arteries, eg, vascular wall edema, perivascular fibrosis, vascular sclerosis, and subendothelial cell damage as a common pathogenic mechanism for all the changes. These changes in turn result in ischemia which, if severe and prolonged enough, would lead to the clinical manifestation of alcoholic cardiomyopathy. The vascular changes occur at a later time than the appearance of structural damage to the mitochondria, sarcoplasmic reticulum, myofibrils, etc. Possible etiologic considerations in the development of the intramyocardial small vessel disease include a direct toxic effect of ethanol and/or acetaldehyde and alcohol-related indirect effects such as acetaldehyde and myocardial catecholamines and altered cardiac magnesium.

Safe levels of alcohol ingestion have not been established in regard to the cardiotoxicity of this drug; however, it has been estimated that it requires 80 g of ethanol per day (equivalent to six standard drinks) over a period of several years to produce a clinically apparent cardiomyopathy in persons without underlying organic heart disease.

Alcoholic cardiomyopathy covers a broad spectrum of signs and symptoms and exists to different degrees of severity; early diagnosis is critical for a favorable prognosis. The following are early manifestations of this disease:

1. Regular consumption of excessive amounts of alcohol for many years (approximately 10 to 15).
2. Complaints of shortness of breath with exertion, palpitations, and paroxysmal nocturnal dyspnea.
3. Persistent sinus tachycardia and an elevated resting systolic blood pressure.
4. Alteration of systolic time intervals, eg, a prolonged pre-ejection period (PEP) and an increased pre-ejection period (PEP)/left ventricular ejection time (LVET) in the resting state and following exercise when compared with nonalcoholic controls.
5. Marked decrease in exercise tolerance.
6. Although EKG changes may be absent in the earlier phases, the following (in association with the history and other signs and symptoms) are suggestive even though the person is asymptomatic: sinus tachycardia; nonspecific S-T-T wave changes; multifocal extra systoles; T-P phenomenon, eg, a prolongation of the S-T segment so that the P wave is inscribed before the T wave returns to the isoelectric line.
7. Abnormal liver function tests.
8. Prominent hilar vascular shadows on chest x-ray, with little or no congestion in the peripheral lung fields.

More advanced forms are seen in patients with overall congestive heart failure, often accompanied by atrial fibrillation, congestion of peripheral lung fields, S-T segment depression, bundle branch block, generalized (biventricular) cardiac enlargement, prominent venous distention and pulse in the neck, gallop rhythm, systolic murmur of either mitral or tricuspid insufficiency, significantly abnormal liver function tests, and hypesthesia and paresthesia, particularly in the lower extremities.

Abstinence from alcohol is the foundation of treatment for all cases of alcoholic cardiomyopathy regardless of severity. Frequently, this will interrupt the progression and even reverse the disease in its earlier forms. Frank congestive heart failure is managed conventionally; however, the prognosis in alcoholic cardiomyopathy is generally considered to be more grave than in cases of congestive failure from other causes.

Coronary Artery Disease. There is considerable historical and current documentation of the negative association between heavy drinking, alcoholism, and occlusion of the large coronary arteries. Recent findings suggest a coronary obstruction-limiting effect of alcohol independent of other coronary risk factors such as hypertension, heavy smoking, and triglyceridemia, all of which are associated with heavy alcohol use. A popular speculation is that the apparent "protective" effect of alcohol on the development of coronary heart disease is due to the fact that alcohol use is associated with increased levels of high-density lipoproteins, which reportedly prevent and possibly reverse the coronary atherogenic process. It should be noted that there may be extensive intramyocardial small vessel pathology associated with heavy drinking even in the absence of large vessel pathology. In view of this, there is currently insufficient evidence to propose that alcohol is "protective" and thus beneficial to cardiac functioning, ameliorating cardiac mortality and morbidity.

Cardiac Arrythmias. Clinical case reports indicate that the *use* and occasional over-use of alcohol can, in some instances, produce transient arrythmias, namely paroxysmal atrial tachycardia, atrial fibrillation, atrial and ventricular ectopic beats, and sinus tachycardia in individuals who are not alcoholics and who have no organic heart disease ("the holiday heart"). If underlying heart disease is present, these conduction disturbances occur more regularly. The EKG changes of alcoholic cardiomyopathy are described above.

Angina and Myocardial Infarction. Recent studies have suggested an inverse relationship between alcohol use and myocardial infarction. This inverse relationship appears to be slightly progressive with consumption of six or more drinks per day; however, the most striking difference in the risk for myocardial infarction is between nondrinkers and those who consume two drinks or fewer per day, with the latter group showing a diminished incidence for major coronary events. Extreme caution must be used in interpreting these data; although there may be agreement that "moderate" drinking is associated with reduced incidence of heart attacks, this does not prevail with "problem" drinkers and alcoholics. Necroscopic evidence has shown that alcoholics who die a cardiac death frequently have a transmural myocardial scar; however, there is no clinical history of a myocardial infarction and no significant coronary (large vessel) atherosclerosis. The intramyocardial small artery disease associated with cardiac myopathy described previously could conceivably compromise appropriate cardiac nutrition, especially in high blood flow requirement situations, so that "atypical" and subclinical myocardial infarctions might occur more frequently than previously suspected. Another possible explanation of myocardial infarction without coronary atherosclerosis in heavy drinkers and alcoholics is external constriction of coronary vessels by scarring due to an underlying cardiomyopathy.

Classical angina is unusual with alcoholic cardiomyopathy and with the atypical myocardial infarction observed in alcoholics. The Prinzemetal variant of angina allegedly caused by large vessel coronary vasospasm can be induced and exacerbated by alcohol. There does not appear to be any rationale for the prescription of alcohol in patients with angina.

Effect of Alcohol on the Peripheral Circulation: Physiological Considerations

A limited number of studies on the hemodynamic impact of ethanol on the peripheral circulation (pressure–volume–flow relationship) suggest that ethanol exerts either no effect, a hypodynamic effect, or a hyperdynamic effect. The conflicting data result from a number of differences in methodology, doses of alcohol, choice of experimental subjects, level of anesthesia, presence or absence of cardiovascular disease, etc. It has been assumed that any acute or chronic drastic change in peripheral hemodynamics caused by alcohol is primarily a reflection of the action on the central circulation.

For many years, a presumed effect of alcohol has been a vasodilatory action, particularly involving the circulation of the skin. There appears to be a distinct difference in this regard, depending on whether or not alcohol is ingested orally or infused IV. Intraarterial alcohol causes constriction of the arterioles of the skin and skeletal muscle; this vasoconstrictive action is not abolished by either sympathectomy or prior treatment with phenoxybenzamine. That data suggest that ethanol per se exerts a direct vasoconstrictive influence on the arteriolar beds of both skin and muscle. When alcohol is given orally, vasodilation of arterioles supplying the skin is observed, with a concomitant vasoconstriction of vessels supplying the corresponding muscle mass. Thus, the vasodilating properties of alcohol appear to be mediated through central reflex phenomena involving neural vasomotor regulatory centers; the vasoconstricting action may be due to a direct effect on arterioles. Another postulate is that alcohol's action is totally vasoconstrictive; the vasodilation occurs because of the peripheral and/or central effects of acetaldehyde.

There is little information concerning morphological changes in the peripheıal vasculature due to acute and chronic exposure to alcohol. In view of the effect of alcohol on intramyocardial small vessels and of the secondary consequences of acute and chronic alcohol consumption such as hyperosmolality, intracellular metabolic changes, Na^+ retention, transcellular electrolyte shifts, and the central and possibly peripheral release and depletion of catecholamines, it is attractive to speculate that some structural changes do occur, particularly at the arteriolar and capillary levels. The growing awareness of the association of heavy drinking, alcoholism, and hypertension demands further research and clinical correlation.

Effect of Alcohol on the Peripheral Circulation: Pathophysiological Considerations

Cerebral Vascular Accident. There is currently a suspicion that a positive relationship exists between heavy alcohol use and stroke, with the hemorrhagic type predominating over the thrombotic type. This relationship appears to be at least in part independent of hypertension. The direct effect of alcohol on platelet function and the indirect hemostatic effects secondary to liver dysfunction may be of some importance.

Hypertension. For years, alcohol use has either been prescribed or certainly not discouraged as a means of treating or even preventing hypertension. Early epidemiological studies failed to demonstrate an association between hypertension and alcohol use; however, these studies were not designed with an appreciation of or sensitivity to different levels of alcohol use.

Hypertension is known to be associated with alcohol abstinence syndrome. Frequently, blood pressure remains elevated and labile for two to three weeks after cessation of drinking, during which time clinically significant signs and symptoms of withdrawal are absent. Thereafter, with abstinence, blood pressure returns to normal. Alcohol-induced hypertension could be due to a number of factors associated with heavy drinking, such as Na^+ retention and an increase in circulating catecholamines. Reversible alcohol-induced hypertension should not be mistaken for essential hypertension (hypertensive vascular disease), since abstinence from alcohol or a dramatic change in the drinking pattern are curative, thus obviating the need for antihypertensive medication.

Recent, more sophisticated, epidemiologic studies designed to assess the morbidity of alcohol consumption reveal increasingly convincing evidence that an association does exist between the regular and substantial use of alcohol and clinically significant elevations in blood pressure.

Data indicate that mean blood pressures in a drinking population that consumed two or fewer drinks per day were similar to the pressures of nondrinkers. However, persons consuming three or more drinks per day had higher systolic and diastolic pressures than did nondrinkers or moderate drinkers (two or fewer drinks per day). This positive correlation continued to increase in Caucasian men and women up to the consumption of six to eight drinks per day, but not above this level.

The association between alcohol use and elevated blood pressure appears to be "independent of age, sex, race, cigarette smoking, coffee use, past heavy drinking, adiposity, educational attainment, or regular salt use." Thus, although there is no unequivocal proof that alcohol use of more than two drinks daily causes hypertension, the current evidence certainly suggests a strong possibility. The diagnostic and management implications for hypertensive individuals who use alcohol should be carefully considered by the treating physician.

In view of recent information concerning cardiovascular mortality and morbidity associated with alcohol, it is difficult not to appreciate the direct and indirect toxicity of this drug on the central and peripheral circulatory systems. Future basic and clinical research in this area is certainly pertinent to the diagnosis, treatment, and prevention of both cardiovascular disease and alcoholism, which rank first and third, respectively, as the major causes of mortality and morbidity in this country.

Liver

Second to the CNS, the liver is the most sensitive organ to the effects of alcohol, largely because the liver metabolizes 90% of ingested alcohol.[9] The most common and usually subclinical form of hepatic dysfunction caused by ethanol is a fatty liver. Alcohol-induced changes of lipid metabolism result in the accumulation (primarily) of triglycerides in the hepatic parenchymal cell. Fatty metamorphosis with serum enzyme elevations can be detected in the asymptomatic, self-proclaimed "social drinker." Modest elevations of serum glutamic-oxaloacetic transaminase (SGOT) (80 to 150) and GGTP (80 to 250) should alert the physician to the strong possibility of alcohol's etiologic role. This condition is probably not precirrhotic, and is readily reversible within 30 days or less with abstinence from alcohol and adequate nutrition. Physical signs include a slightly enlarged hepar, which is usually nontender to palpation; return to a normal-size liver occurs with recovery.

Alcoholic hepatitis is a more serious and clinically symptomatic condition than fatty liver. This disorder can be an acute or chronic inflammation of the liver that is characterized by marked parenchymal cell necrosis; in some cases, it is reversible, but it is the most common cause of cirrhosis in the United States, and women apparently are more susceptible than men. Generally, the incidence is related to the duration (10 to 15 years or more) and the amount (>160 g ethanol per day) of the drinking pattern. Anorexia, nausea, vomiting, hepatomegaly, and jaundice strongly suggest the diagnosis; abdominal pain and tenderness, splenomegaly, ascites, fever, and encephalopathy support the diagnosis. Although the SGOT may be normal in 15% to 25% of the cases, if elevated, values are usually <300 mU/mL. Elevations of alkaline phosphatase are common; hyperbilirubinemia occurs in 60% to 90% of the cases. A progressive prolongation of the prothombin time is associated with a grave prognosis. Nutritional therapy and abstinence from alcohol are the cornerstones of treatment. There is evidence that the progression of this disease is in part an immunological phenomenon; however, the effectiveness of corticosteroids has not been established and is equivocal at best. In persons who appear to recover from acute alcoholic hepatitis, the mortality rate over the next three-year period is ten times greater than that of nonalcohol-dependent individuals of comparable age.

Cirrhosis ranks seventh among the leading causes of death in the United States and has traditionally been associated with alcoholism. It is noteworthy that of all persons who die from cirrhosis, 90% are alcohol-dependent; however, only ≤ 10% of alcohol-dependent persons suffer from cirrhosis. Previous speculation that alcohol per se can cause cirrhosis is resolving. Alcohol-dependent persons can develop cirrhosis in one (or possibly a combination) of four ways. First, Laennec's type of cirrhosis, associated with severe malnutrition, is exacerbated by alcohol. Second cirrhosis (mainly postnecrotic type), which results from combined hepatotoxic insults, occurs most commonly in persons suffering viral hepatitis who drink ethanol. No patient with viral hepatitis should drink alcohol; any person who has clinically recovered from viral hepatitis and remains antigen-positive should be advised to abstain from alcohol. Any person who has had clinically significant viral hepatitis, who recovers without antigenicity, and who chooses to use alcohol should have liver function tests performed on a regular basis. Third, recent research results suggest that if a sufficient number of a person's daily calories (≥ 50%) is consumed daily as ethanol for a long enough period of time (five years or longer), there is an increased risk of cirrhosis without any apparent associated malnutrition. Fourth, cirrhosis can develop as a malignant progression of alcoholic hepatitis.

There is now evidence that alcohol *alone* as a direct hepatotoxin can cause fatty liver, alcoholic hepatitis, and cirrhosis, regardless of the state of nutrition. However, many other variables that affect susceptibility, such as genetic, endocrine, and immunological factors, demand further investigation.

Pancreas

Acute pancreatitis is strongly associated with excessive alcohol consumption (50% of cases).[9] However, subclinical pancreatic damage, often asymptomatic and frequently underdiagnosed, is much more common and is responsible for a covert state of malnutrition, eg, carbohydrate intolerance and malabsorption, particularly of fat and vitamins. The pathogenesis of alcohol-induced pancreatitis is not well understood, but a number of factors may be operational. Alcohol leads to an increase in pancreatic secretion and contraction of the sphincter of Oddi (with or without duodenal irritation). Pancreatic secretions extravasate into the interstitial tissue and directly damage acinar cells. Alcohol also causes an inspissation of pancreatic secretion in the smaller ducts which, with continued alcohol use, progresses. In addition, high-fat and high-protein diets seem to predispose the heavy drinker to alcoholic pancreatitis.

Conventional treatment approaches to pancreatitis usually result in remission; however, treatment of the individual's alcohol abuse/dependence, including abstinence from alcohol, is essential in preventing relapses.

Gastrointestinal Tract[10]

Esophagus

Dyspepsia and "heartburn" are very common complaints treated by the practicing physician. Excessive alcohol use impairs peristalsis in the distal third of the esophagus and causes an impaired peristaltic response to deglutition, thus increasing the likelihood of reflux esophagitis. Alcohol abuse/dependence should be suspected in persons presenting with recurrent and/or refractory heartburn symptoms.

Stomach

Depending on the concentration of ethanol, significant amounts of this drug can be absorbed directly by the stomach (25% to 40% of an ingested amount of alcohol). At the same time, alcohol interferes with gastric motility and emptying while increasing gastric secretion, which is high in acid and low in pepsin content. These phenomena can lead to hyperemia, hemorrhage, erosion, and ulceration of the gastric mucosa, causing the clinical signs and symptoms of acute gastritis. The diagnostic subterfuge of "acute gastritis" as admission and discharge diagnoses to general hospitals is often only a symptom of alcohol abuse/dependence that must be recognized and treated.

Small Intestine

The effect of acute and chronic alcohol use on small intestine function has been observed clinically for many years. Changes in motility may well account for the diarrhea often seen in alcohol-dependent patients. The physician should suspect alcohol use as an etiologic or exacerbating factor in anyone who complains of recurrent, chronic, or refractory diarrhea. Structural changes occur in small intestinal mucosa with chronic excessive use of alcohol, leading to malabsorption of vitamins and various nutrients.

Musculoskeletal System

Early clinical observations (ca 1837) suggested that chronic excessive use of alcohol in some persons resulted in a progressive weakness of the limbs, a condition which was generally reversible with discontinuation of alcohol use.[11] Initially, the myopathy and acute and chronic myositis associated with chronic alcohol dependence was thought to be secondary to a primary neuropathy; recent observations in this regard have demonstrated by electromyography and muscle biopsy several forms of alcoholic myopathy.

Acute alcoholic myopathy, the least frequent yet most serious of these forms, usually follows an alcoholic debauch, often in conjunction with strenuous exercise. Clinically, these patients present with weakness (with or without paralysis) and acute muscular pain—usually of the proximal limb musculature; these symptoms may be accompanied by a rapidly progressive rhabdomyolysis with myoglobinuria, hyperkalemia, renal failure, and death. Usually signs and symptoms disappear with cessation of alcohol intake and adequate nutrition, particularly a high-carbohydrate diet.

Subclinical alcoholic myopathy is probably the most common form and is frequently diagnosed on the basis of elevated creatine phosphokinase (CPK), SGOT, LDH-1 and LDH-2 levels in the serum. There may be no clinical signs or symptoms; often, however, the patient complains of a generalized muscular weakness and a significant decrease in exercise tolerance.

Chronic alcoholic myopathy is insidious in onset and development and involves symmetrical weakness with or without atrophy of the proximal musculature of the lower extremities. Frequently, a drinking episode may precipitate an acute myopathy superimposed on a chronic process.

The pathogenesis of alcoholic myopathy is still somewhat controversial, but is thought to result from one or a combination of factors: (a) direct toxicity of ethanol and its metabolites, ie, acetaldehyde; (b) nutritional deficiencies, especially carbohydrate; and (c) phosphate deficiency.

Treatment approaches that embrace strenuous exercise as a requisite for "conditioning" should be planned with caution for persons suffering alcoholic myopathy. Abstinence from alcohol and adequate nutrition provide significant relief and often complete reversal of the alcohol-induced myopathic process.

Hematopoietic System

The direct and indirect effects of alcohol on the hematopoietic system frequently result in significant clinical disorders, primarily anemia, hemorrhagic diathesis, and increased susceptibility to infection.[12,13]

Anemia

The anemias associated with chronic alcohol dependence are usually mild and varied and can include normocytic, microcytic, or macrocytic types; they can be normochromic, hypochromic, or hyperchromic, depending on the predominant pathophysiologic process.

The anemias result from one or a combination of many alcohol-induced abnormalities, such as liver disease; direct suppression of erythropoiesis; real and functional folate deficiencies due to decreased intake, absorption, hepatic storage, and cellular metabolism of folate; blood loss; and hypersplenism.

In the subacute phase of alcohol dependence, the most significant factor is probably a suppression of erythropoiesis, which involves abnormal iron and folate metabolism and an inhibition of heme synthesis. Erythrocyte macrocytosis is quite common; an otherwise unexplained elevated mean corpuscular volume (MCV) is a reasonably reliable hematologic indicator for excessive alcohol use.

Hemorrhagic Diathesis

Alcohol-induced blood loss, usually occult and insidious, results from decreased platelet production and aggregation, bleeding from esophagitis, and gastritis and liver disease that interfere with coagulation.

Increased Susceptibility to Infection

Respiratory tract infection, particularly the pneumonias, is among the most clinically significant infections seen in alcohol-dependent persons. Other infections that occur with increased frequency include meningitis, septic arthritis, skin infections, tuberculosis, septicemia, and peritonitis. Chronic alcohol use causes a decreased production and impaired chemotaxis of granulocytes and a decreased plasma bacteriacidal activity. These consequences, coupled with personal neglect often seen in heavy drinkers, create an infectious diathesis. Recurrent and/or refractory infections should alert the physician to the possibility that these may be clinical manifestations of an underlying drinking problem. Because of the impaired immune response, infections in alcohol-dependent patients should be appropriately treated in an early and aggressive manner.

PSYCHOLOGICAL DYSFUNCTION

Of the many psychological or emotional problems affecting patients, four common complaints that are often associated with underlying subacute alcohol dependency are anxiety, depression, sleep disturbance, and sexual dysfunction.

Although these complaints may be associated with a psychiatric illness, the physician frequently hears statements such as: "Doctor, I drink because I'm anxious (depressed), (can't sleep), (have a bad sex life)." In many cases, these problems are actually a result of excessive alcohol use rather than the presumed cause. The physician should bear this in mind during attempts to ascertain the presence or absence of any significant psychopathology associated with alcohol dependence.

The practicing physician sees the subacute phase of alcohol abuse/dependence in conjunction with various conditions common in everyday medical practice. Recognition of the etiologic and/or complicating and/or exacerbating roles played by alcohol use in these conditions will allow the physician to practice effective secondary prevention, ie, to treat the apparent medical-psychiatric disorder and also to intervene in the destructive drinking pattern at an earlier stage.

REFERENCES

1. Beard JD, Knott DH: The effect of alcohol on fluid and electrolyte metabolism, in Kissin B, Begleiter H (eds): *The Biology of Alcoholism: I Biochemistry.* New York, Plenum, 1971, pp 353–376.
2. Knott DH: Alcoholism: A complex clinical syndrome. *Hosp Med* 1979; 15:50–58.
3. Johnson RB, Lukash MW: Medical complications of alcohol abuse. Summary of 1973 AMA Washington Conference, AMA Publication No. MH1530-436K, 7-25M, 1974, pp 17–21.
4. Hillman R: Alcoholism and malnutrition, in Kissin B, Begleiter H (eds): *The Biology of Alcoholism: III Clinical Pathology.* New York, Plenum, 1974, pp 513–560.
5. Dreyfus PM: Diseases of the nervous system in chronic alcoholics, in Kissin B, Begleiter H (eds): *The Biology of Alcoholism: III Clinical Pathology.* New York, Plenum, 1974, pp 265–286.
6. Lyons SA, Saltzman A: Diseases of the respiratory tract in alcoholics, in Kissin B, Begleiter H (eds): *The Biology of Alcoholism: III Clinical Pathology.* New York, Plenum, 1974, pp 403–431.
7. Bing RJ, Tillmans H: The effect of alcohol on the heart, in Lieber CS (ed): *Metabolic Aspects of Alcoholism.* Lancaster, MTP, 1977, pp 117–134.
8. Knott DH, Beard JD: Effects of alcohol ingestion on the cardiovascular system, in Pattison EM, Kaufman E (eds): *Encyclopedic Handbook of Alcoholism.* New York, Gardner, 1982, pp 332–342.
9. Korsten MA, Lieber CS: Liver and pancreas, in Pattison EM, Kaufman E (eds): *Encyclopedic Handbook of Alcoholism.* New York, Gardner, 1982, pp 225–244.
10. Lorber SH, Dinoso VP, Chey WY: Diseases of the gastrointestinal tract, in Kissin B, Begleiter H (eds): *The Biology of Alcoholism: III Clinical Pathology.* New York, Plenum, 1974, pp 339–357.
11. Ferguson ER, Knochel JP: Myopathy in the chronic alcoholic, in Pattison EM, Kaufman E (eds): *Encyclopedic Handbook of Alcoholism.* New York, Gardner, 1982, pp 204–214.
12. Lindenbaum J: Metabolic effects of alcohol on the blood and bone marrow, in Lieber CS (ed): *Metabolic Aspects of Alcoholism.* Lancaster, MTP, 1977, pp 215–248.
13. Chanarin I: Effects of alcohol on the hematopoietic system, in Pattison EM, Kaufman E (eds): *Encyclopedic Handbook of Alcoholism.* New York, Gardner, 1982, pp 332–342.

Chapter 5
DIAGNOSIS

The single unitary disease concept of alcoholism is fraught with diagnostic and treatment problems for the practicing physician. The alcoholisms (alcohol-dependence syndrome) and the alcohol-related disabilities phenomenologically permit more diagnostic flexibility and latitude.[1,2] To reiterate from Chapter 1, alcohol-dependence syndrome represents a group of disorders, at the core of which are tolerance to and physical dependency on ethyl alcohol. This syndrome is of multidimensional origin; can be mild, moderate, or severe; or intermittent or continuous; it can undergo clinical remission with treatment (this occasionally is spontaneous), and can result in progressive deterioration and death.

Alcohol-related disabilities are disorders that involve impairment in the performance of activities which, in accordance with the subject's age, sex, and normative social role, are generally accepted as essential basic concepts of daily living, such as self-care, social relations and economic activity. Alcohol-related disabilities may or may not coexist with alcohol-dependence syndrome; disability may be short-term, long-term, or permanent. There can be clinical remission (with treatment or spontaneous), and the disabilities can result in progressive deterioration and death.

It is important that diagnosis (a) determine whether or not alcohol dependence syndrome exists concomitantly with alcohol-related disabilities; (b) define operationally the types of and extent of alcohol-related disabilities; and (c) describe critical physiological, psychological, social, and environmental variables that either exacerbate or ameliorate alcohol-dependence syndrome and/or the alcohol-related disabilities.

HISTORY

A complete history should always include a careful alcohol and drug assessment in terms of alcohol use. Certain questions should not be asked, such as: Do you drink? How much do you drink? How frequently do you drink? What do you drink? and How long have you been drinking? Such questions are frequently perceived by the patient as being judgmental; the reply often

Is, "I only have a couple of beers once in a while." In addition, it has been well demonstrated that a person's recollection of consumption/frequency patterns is poor; often there is an underestimate of alcohol use. Fortunately, recent trends do not consider the issue of how much, how often, or how long to be the sine qua non of diagnosis; rather, the impact that alcohol has on the individual's health (physical, psychological, social) is more important, regardless of frequency or quantity indices.

Although there are many interview techniques that can be used, I have found the following plan of inquiry to be useful with persons who are seen for evaluation or treatment, especially when a "drinking problem" may not be immediately evident.

Begin by evaluating the patient's use of prescribed drugs, saying, "I would like to discuss with you medications which you are taking that have been prescribed by a doctor." The use of the term "medicine" rather than "drugs" is less provocative. This portion of the patient's history should include the past and current use of all drugs, ie, psychotropics, antibiotics, antihistamines, antispasmodics, etc. The patient is usually truthful about the use of prescribed medications; furthermore, the physician can gain some appreciation of the drug orientation of the patient, ie, whether the patient is one who truly believes in "better living through chemistry."

Second, determine the patient's use of proprietary drugs, saying, "Now I would like to discuss with you the medications which you buy from the drugstore or those recommended by your pharmacist for which you do not need a prescription." It may take a few minutes to make the patient understand that over-the-counter medications are indeed drugs, with significant effects and side effects.

Last, say to the patient, "Finally, I would like to discuss with you the medications which you prescribe for yourself."

Invariably, the patient will deny the use of any drug not prescribed by either a physician or a pharmacist. Begin by exploring the patient's use of such drugs as caffeine and nicotine, explaining that these are "medications" with specific effects, especially on the CNS. The dialogue can then continue:

Physician: "What about the sedatives (tranquilizers) you prescribe for yourself?"

Patient: "I don't use any tranquilizers that are not prescribed by a doctor or that are not available in the drugstore."

Physician: "I would like to know how alcohol makes you feel. You know that alcohol is a sedative, or tranquilizer, and it has very specific effects on the nervous system. I'm wondering what effects it has on your nervous system."

Discuss the effects that alcohol has on the particular patient and ascertain the circumstances and the setting in which alcohol use occurs. It is especially important to determine how rapidly the patient ingests alcohol (gulper v sipper), since, in many instances, alcohol-related pathophysiology and psychopathology are related to how high the blood alcohol concentration (BAC) is and how often such levels are achieved. Questioning should be nonmoralistic and nonjudgmental and designed to discover how important the individual perceives the drug, ethyl alcohol, to be in regard to his or her daily functioning.

The physician can assume that between 60% to 70% of the adult population in this country consumes alcohol for purposes other than strictly religious. The emphasis on taking the history is to establish that the patient *uses* alcohol and then to determine whether alcohol dependence syndrome and/or alcohol-related disabilities exist.

PSYCHOLOGICAL FACTORS: MENTAL STATUS EXAMINATION

Four of the most common psychological complaints heard by physicians in their office and hospital practice are: anxiety, hyperirritability ("nerves"); insomnia; sadness (feeling "blue" — depression); and sexual dysfunction.

Although the chronic heavy use of alcohol may be the cause of these problems, the patient will frequently state, "I drink because my nerves are bad." (anxiety and depression); or "I can't sleep, and I have a lousy sex life." If indeed these psychological complaints are due to alcohol, they will disappear or dramatically decrease in intensity with 30 days' abstinence from alcohol.

Although many busy physicians do not include a mental status examination in the diagnostic evaluation, this tool can be extremely helpful in discovering early forms of alcohol-dependence syndrome and/or alcohol-related disabilities.[3] Even though there is no pathognomonic mental status of the alcohol-dependent person, the following are common findings that can increase the index of suspicion of alcohol-related disorders.

Appearance, attitude and general behavior. In physical appearance, the alcohol-dependent person: appears older than chronological age; lacks a certain degree of cooperation, ie, is often negativistic; and in general activity is hyperactive, tremulous, and agitated.

Stream of mental activity ("verbal behavior"). The alcohol-dependent person often has spontaneous productive speech. The progression of thought is usually coherent and relevant, but occasionally a response may not be pertinent to the question.

Emotional tone and reactions. Affect of the alcohol-dependent person is appropriate, but frequently is characterized by depression, unhappiness, and sadness; affect may be labile, ranging from elation to depression during the interview; dysphoria, anxiety, and anger are also common.

Mental trend and thought content. Alcohol-dependent persons often have multiple somatic complaints and ideas of reference. With regard to sensorium, mental grasp, and capacity, the patient is oriented, but often exhibits deficits in recent memory, impaired judgment, diminished attention span and concentration, and an inability to think abstractly.

Disorders of mental status reflect the cortical dysfunction that can be consequent to chronic alcohol use.

Physiological Factors[3,4]

Past Medical History

Although certainly not exhaustive, the following list of medical disorders may, if elicited as part of the past medical history, suggest alcohol-related disabilities that have been avoided, ignored, or misdiagnosed.

1. Recurrent and/or refractory edema
2. Hypoglycemia
3. Gout
4. Hyperlipidemia
5. Peripheral neuropathy
6. Recurrent episodes of bronchitis
7. Recurrent episodes of bacterial and viral pneumonia
8. Aspiration pneumonia
9. Fractured ribs
10. Bronchiectasis
11. Lung abscess
12. Hypertension
13. Cardiac failure
14. Cardiac arrythmias
15. Liver dysfunction
16. Pancreatitis
17. Gastritis
18. Esophagitis
19. Malabsorption syndromes
20. Colitis
21. Acute or chronic myopathy
22. Anemia

Physical Examination

Although myriad physical manifestations of alcohol use can exist, there are certain findings on physical examination which are not necessarily pathognomonic but which can be presumptive for the earlier forms of the alcohol-related disorders when considered in the context of the history, mental status examination, and past medical history.

A. HEENT (head, eyes, ears, nose, throat)
1. Suffused conjunctive
2. Premature arcus senilis
3. Nystagmus
4. Periorbital edema
5. Toxic amblyopia
6. Facial telangiectasia
7. Bilateral parotid gland enlargement
8. Flushed facies
9. Tongue — dry; trembling; edges are irregular; papillae blunted or obliterated
10. Pharyngeal hyperemia
B. Chest
1. Signs of bronchitis (frequently refractory to treatment)
2. Emphysema and chronic obstructive pulmonary disease (at an earlier than expected age)
3. Rib fractures
C. Cardiovascular
1. Systolic and diastolic hypertension
2. Labile blood pressure with serial measurements
3. Sinus tachycardia (persistent)
4. Cardiac arrythmias
D. Abdomen
1. Obesity — frequently increased adipose tissue in the abdominal wall without a generalized total body distribution of fatty tissue
2. Hepatomegaly — frequently nontender to palpation
3. Epigastric tenderness to palpation
E. Extremities
1. Tremors
2. Ecchymosis — particularly significant if patient cannot recall the cause
3. Cigarette stains or burns on fingers
4. Hyperreflexia
5. Hypesthesia
6. Muscle tenderness
7. Edema

Interpretation of Laboratory Parameters

Certain biochemical abnormalities caused by alcohol use can exist prior to clinically ostentatious physical, psychological, or social deterioration, and can assist the physician in making an earlier diagnosis. It should be noted that laboratory abnormalities are diagnostic clues but in and of themselves do not necessarily form the foundation for the diagnosis of alcohol-dependence syndrome.

Interpretation of the laboratory data must be considered within the context of the alcohol/drug history, past medical history, mental status examination, and physical examination.

1. Liver dysfunction—especially elevated SGOT and GGTP
2. Hematopoietic
   a. Elevation in mean corpuscular volume (MCV)
   b. Anemia, microcytic, normocytic, and macrocytic
   c. Leukopenia
   d. Thrombocytopenia
3. Hyperlipidemia (especially type IV) (elevated HDL > 60)
4. Hyperuricemia
5. Hypophosphatemia
6. Hypoglycemia on glucose tolerance test
7. Carbohydrate intolerance on glucose tolerance test
8. Hypomagnesia
9. Elevated serum amylase/lipase
10. Urinalysis
    a. Persistent hyposthenuria
    b. Asymptomatic pyuria
    c. Increased incidence of urinary tract infections
    d. Albuminuria

Some of the significant metabolic abnormalities, systemic effects of alcohol, and physical findings are summarized in Figures 5.1, 5.2, and 5.3, respectively.

The above discussion pertains primarily to the patient who seeks medical assistance for a variety of medical and psychological problems and who is either unaware of or denies the role that alcohol use might be playing in past and current illnesses. Once the above information has been collated, the physician is afforded the opportunity to make the diagnosis of alcohol-dependence syndrome (alcoholisms) and/or alcohol-related disabilities. The next approach to be considered is illustrated by the following case history and the subsequent physician–patient interaction.

Case History

John Doe, a 40-year-old, employed (bank vice president) Caucasian man with three children (ages 10, 14, and 16 years) was seen at his family physician's office for his "annual checkup." His primary complaint was "heartburn," postprandial epigastric distress; he last visited his physician two years

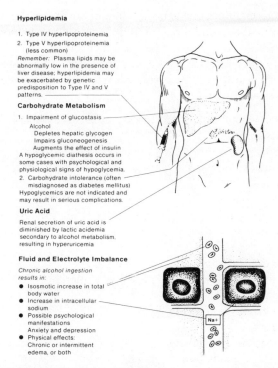

Hyperlipidemia

1. Type IV hyperlipoproteinemia
2. Type V hyperlipoproteinemia
   (less common)
Remember: Plasma lipids may be abnormally low in the presence of liver disease; hyperlipidemia may be exacerbated by genetic predisposition to Type IV and V patterns.

Carbohydrate Metabolism

1. Impairment of glucostasis
   Alcohol
     Depletes hepatic glycogen
     Impairs gluconeogenesis
     Augments the effect of insulin
   A hypoglycemic diathesis occurs in some cases with psychological and physiological signs of hypoglycemia.
2. Carbohydrate intolerance (often misdiagnosed as diabetes mellitus) Hypoglycemics are not indicated and may result in serious complications.

Uric Acid

Renal secretion of uric acid is diminished by lactic acidemia secondary to alcohol metabolism, resulting in hyperuricemia

Fluid and Electrolyte Imbalance

Chronic alcohol ingestion results in:
● Isosmotic increase in total body water
● Increase in intracellular sodium
● Possible psychological manifestations
  Anxiety and depression
● Physical effects:
  Chronic or intermittent edema, or both

Figure 5.1. Metabolic abnormalities in alcohol dependence, some common pathophysiologic states that can be recognized before advanced stages of alcoholism become manifest. Adapted from Knott DH: Alcoholism: A complex clinical syndrome. *Hosp Med* 15:50–65, 1979.

ago for evaluation of elevated blood pressure which subsequently stabilized without medication.

The patient states that he takes an occasional antihistamine (three to four times per year) for a "cold". Use of aspirin has increased during the past year for headaches (12 aspirin tablets/week). The patient considers himself a "social drinker," stating "Alcohol relaxes me after a hard day." Patient further reveals having "two drinks before dinner on a daily basis" but denies being intoxicated. Patient has negative family history for any serious medical disorders, psychiatric disorders, or alcohol or drug problems.

From a psychological viewpoint, the patient describes increased job pressures for the past year, with little time left for previously satisfactory family activities. Further complaints include middle-to-late insomnia, hyperirritability, and a loss of interest in sex ("I'm always too tired."). Mental status examination was essentially normal except that affect was depressed, and pa-

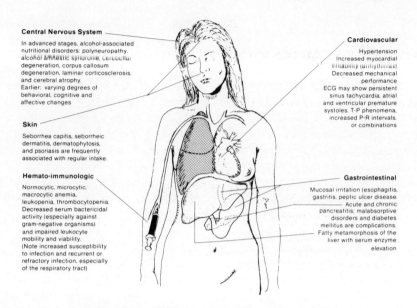

Central Nervous System

In advanced stages, alcohol-associated nutritional disorders: polyneuropathy, alcohol amnestic syndrome, cerebellar degeneration, corpus callosum degeneration, laminar corticosclerosis, and cerebral atrophy. Earlier: varying degrees of behavioral, cognitive and affective changes

Skin

Seborrhea capitis, seborrheic dermatitis, dermatophytosis, and psoriasis are frequently associated with regular intake.

Hemato-immunologic

Normocytic, microcytic, macrocytic anemia, leukopenia, thrombocytopenia. Decreased serum bactericidal activity (especially against gram-negative organisms) and impaired leukocyte mobility and viability. (Note increased susceptibility to infection and recurrent or refractory infection, especially of the respiratory tract)

Cardiovascular

Hypertension Increased myocardial irritability (arrhythmias) Decreased mechanical performance ECG may show persistent sinus tachycardia, atrial and ventricular premature systoles, T-P phenomena, increased P-R intervals, or combinations

Gastrointestinal

Mucosal irritation (esophagitis, gastritis, peptic ulcer disease. Acute and chronic pancreatitis; malabsorptive disorders and diabetes mellitus are complications. Fatty metamorphosis of the liver with serum enzyme elevation

Figure 5.2. Checklist of systemic effects of alcohol. Adapted from Knott DH: Alcoholism: A complex clinical syndrome. *Hosp Med* 15:50–65, 1979.

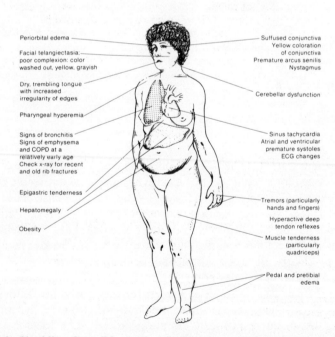

Periorbital edema

Facial telangiectasia; poor complexion: color washed out, yellow, grayish

Dry, trembling tongue with increased irregularity of edges

Pharyngeal hyperemia

Signs of bronchitis Signs of emphysema and COPD at a relatively early age Check x-ray for recent and old rib fractures

Epigastric tenderness

Hepatomegaly

Obesity

Suffused conjunctiva Yellow coloration of conjunctiva Premature arcus senilis Nystagmus

Cerebellar dysfunction

Sinus tachycardia Atrial and ventricular premature systoles ECG changes

Tremors (particularly hands and fingers)

Hyperactive deep tendon reflexes

Muscle tenderness (particularly quadriceps)

Pedal and pretibial edema

Figure 5.3. Checklist of possible physical findings in cases of alcohol abuse. Adapted from Knott DH: Alcoholism: A complex clinical syndrome. *Hosp Med* 15:50–65, 1979.

tient stated that, "My boss and co-workers are trying to make my work more difficult."

Physical examination (positive findings) shows: HEENT, horizontal nystagmus on lateral gaze; cardiovascular, P, 96 with occasional premature ventricular contraction (PVC); blood pressure (BP), 158/98–96 sitting with three different readings; abdomen, slight increase in hepar size, nontender, and epigastric pain to palpation. Pertinent laboratory findings are: EKG, sinus tachycardia with occasional PVC; SGOT, 96; GGTP, 80; and MCV, 101.

The remainder of the physical and laboratory evaluations, complete blood count (CBC), urinalysis, and SMA-18, were within normal limits. The following conversation ensued:

> *Physician:* "John, your examination reveals some things that are bothersome. You have some signs and symptoms of depression (insomnia, hyperirritability, and decreased libido). In addition, your blood pressure and pulse rate are elevated, and there is a slight increase in your liver enzymes as well as in the size of your red blood cells."
>
> *Patient:* "Doctor, if I could only decrease my pressure at work I'd be all right."
>
> *Physician:* "John, the only thing to which I can connect your abnormal findings is possibly your drinking pattern."
>
> *Patient:* "Are you calling me alcoholic? I drink much less than my friends."
>
> *Physician:* "No, I'm not calling you alcoholic, but I do feel you should stop drinking for 30 days, since, if these abnormalities are caused by your use of alcohol, they should disappear in 30 days. Can you stop drinking for 30 days?"
>
> *Patient:* "Of course I can. I can take it or leave it."
>
> *Physician:* "Good—no alcohol for 30 days; please return at that time for re-evaluation. If you drink any alcohol within the next 30 days, please call me, as I would like to discuss this further with you."

One month later, the patient returns:

> *Physician:* "How are you feeling, John?"
>
> *Patient:* "I feel great! I haven't had a drink for a month. I'm sleeping better; I've had sexual intercourse with my wife five times, and my heartburn is gone. Also, I'm able to get my work done in a shorter period of time. The pressure is less."

Reevaluation shows a BP of 130/86-80 and a P of 80 and regular; all of the physical and laboratory abnormalities have disappeared.

> *Physician:* "All of the abnormal findings are now gone."
>
> *Patient:* "I feel better than I've felt in years. Do you think it was the alcohol?"
>
> *Physician:* "It appears that your alcohol use was causing both the physical and psychological problems."
>
> *Patient:* "Can I ever drink again? Am I alcoholic?"
>
> *Physician:* "Your diagnosis involves alcohol-related disabilities, but, at this point, you do not suffer from alcohol-dependence syndrome. I would advise

abstinence for at least another 30 days. Thereafter, if you choose to drink, we can discuss the issue."

Obviously, this is the ideal patient; however, if the physician is willing to recognize and deal very directly with alcohol-related disabilities early in the course of the disease trajectory, outcome and prognosis are excellent.

Unfortunately, not all patients are as compliant or have progressed to more serious forms of alcohol-dependence syndrome/alcohol-related disabilities. If the physician has established effective rapport with the patient in a nonjudgmental, nonmoralistic manner, the patient who cannot stop drinking for 30 days will often call the physician for further help. The role that the physician can play with such a patient is discussed in Chapter 6.

The discussion of diagnosis thus far has involved persons who may be suffering certain alcohol-related disabilities or the subacute phase of alcohol-dependence syndrome and who encounter the health care system for treatment of a variety of physical and psychological problems related to alcohol use. Aggressive intervention that involves dealing directly with the etiologic role of alcohol is simply the practice of secondary prevention.

It is not difficult to diagnose alcohol-dependence syndrome and the more advanced stages of alcohol-related disabilities in persons who present in acute withdrawal or with the chief complaint of, "I'm an alcoholic." The growing number of alcoholism treatment centers within the health care delivery system and the increasing acceptance by the lay public of the idea that alcoholism is a treatable illness provide for easier access to treatment. Thus, the practicing physician is often faced with the self-recognized and clinically evident alcohol-dependent patient. The following is a format I use with such patients in regard to history and interview. Obviously, there are some aspects of this format that should be incorporated in the approach to the subacute patient.

1. Chief Complaint
   a. General description of the patient's condition.
   b. Referral source.
   c. Justification for placing the patient in a restricted environment, (hospital *v* outpatient setting).
   d. Reliability of the patient as a historian or reliability of the person from whom the history is obtained.
2. Alcohol and Drug History
   a. Current history of alcohol and drug use pattern, including an estimation of daily consumption index and frequency. The history should focus first on the primary drug of abuse, but should also include any other drugs — legend or proprietary.
   b. Statement as to when alcohol/drug abuse pattern began and a narrative on the nature of that pattern, eg, intermittent, episodic, continuous, etc.

   c. Statement concerning time when the patient felt alcohol/drugs became a problem and a statement as to when you, the interviewer, felt that the problem began.

   d. Past treatment experiences for alcohol/drug dependence, where, when, by whom, and a statement as to the patient's response to treatment.

   e. A statement as to whether or not the patient is intoxicated, withdrawing from, or psychotic as a consequence of alcohol/drugs at the time of admission.

3. Physiological Description

   a. A general statement describing the physiological status of the patient at the time of admission, particularly in regard to the state of intoxication or withdrawal.

   b. Patient's medical–surgical–psychiatric history.

   c. Review of systems.

   d. Family medical history.

4. Psychological Description

   a. Assessment of premorbid functioning, ie, was psychological functioning normal or abnormal prior to the onset of alcohol/drug dependence; if abnormal, describe the type of dysfunction.

   b. A description of the current psychological status of the patient and a statement concerning the extent to which the psychopathology (if any is noted) appears to be either induced by, mobilized by, or aggravated by alcohol/drug dependence.

   c. Mental status examination.

   d. Family history of alcohol/drug dependence and/or psychiatric disorders, at least in the first-degree and second-degree biological relatives.

5. Social Description

   a. Status of nuclear and extended family including past and current marital status, relationship to biological relatives.

   b. Statement concerning past and current employment status and overall vocational stability and satisfaction.

   c. Description of avocational activities, past and current.

   d. Statement concerning social relationships, eg, low, middle, upper SES, type and nature of social contacts and relationships.

   e. Past and current religious affiliations and activities.

   f. Past and current legal charges, including disposition of these charges, eg, dismissed, indicted, convicted, parole, probation, etc.

The diagnostic approach to alcohol-dependence syndrome/alcohol-related disabilities cannot be a rigid, concretized process, but rather must be a flexible one designed to assess and diagnose at various stages of the diseases of alcoholism. The terms, alcohol-dependence syndrome and alcohol-related disabilities, while compatible with the DSM-III categories of Alcohol Abuse and Alcohol Dependence, do allow more flexibility and individualization of diagnosis.[5] It is imperative that practicing physicians increase their diagnostic acumen for these disorders in order to: (a) ascertain the nature of the diseases of alcoholism; (b) promote early detection; (c) gather data that may ultimately provide a uniform yet dynamic nomenclature; (d) prevent underdiagnosis and overdiagnosis; and (e) provide for individualized treatment approaches.

REFERENCES

1. Criteria Committee of the National Council on Alcoholism: Criteria for the diagnosis of alcoholism. *Am J Psychiatry* 129:127–135, 1972.
2. American Psychiatric Association: *Diagnostic and Statistical Manual of Mental Disorders*, ed 4. Washington DC, APA, 1980.
3. Knott DH,: Alcoholism: A complex clinical syndrome. *Hosp Med* 15:50–65, 1979.
4. Knott DH, Fink RD, Morgan JC: The subacute phase of alcoholism. *Am Fam Physician* 15:108, 1977.
5. Nathan PE: Alcoholism and DSM-III. *Adv Alcoholism* 1980; 1(15).

Chapter 6
THE PHYSICIAN'S ROLE
IN DIAGNOSIS AND TREATMENT
OF THE CHRONIC
PHASE OF ALCOHOL
DEPENDENCE SYNDROME

After physiological stabilization, the chronic phase of alcohol-dependence syndrome occurs. It is a condition associated with psychological, social, family, and vocational problems that may have preceded the onset of alcohol abuse/dependence but is most certainly consequential to it.

The challenges posed for the physician in managing the patient in the chronic phase include[1]: (a) differential diagnosis of alcohol-dependence syndrome (alcoholisms); (b) recognition of and dealing with certain psychological factors such as denial, dependency, depression, and narcissism; (c) psychotherapeutic approaches; (d) chemotherapeutic approaches; (e) referral issues (who, when, where); and (f) prognostic issues (realistic treatment outcome expectations).

DIFFERENTIAL DIAGNOSIS

There is an implicit therapeutic nihilism in considering alcoholism as a single unitary disease entity, since all too often the assumption that there must be a single optimal treatment approach follows. Further diagnostic refinement encourages treatment flexibility and is not necessarily incompatible with other currently accepted phenomenological systems such as Alcohol Abuse and Alcohol Dependence (DSM III) or Alcohol-Dependence Syndrome and Alcohol-related Disabilities (World Health Organization).

A modification of a diagnostic classification has been useful to me in assuming further therapeutic responsibility in the management of patients who are in difficulty with alcohol.[2] Such patients can be divided, albeit at times arbitrarily, into three major categories: primary, secondary, and reactive.

Primary Group

Heretofore, persons suffering from a primary process which leads to alcohol dependence (tolerance and physical dependence) have constituted the largest group seeking and finding treatment. The profile of the primary "alcoholic" generally includes the following characteristics.

There is an early loss of control of alcohol use. The characteristic drinking pattern is usually episodic and involves alcohol use to the extreme with almost every drinking bout. There is seldom a history of drinking without problems for any length of time no matter at what age the onset of drinking occurs. In relating a drinking history, these individuals are usually self-diagnosed alcoholics and will remember vividly the effects of that "first drink." Furthermore, these patients will emphatically state that having only a "couple of drinks" is a struggle, often saying, "If I can only have a drink or two, it's not worth drinking." There is often a positive family history of alcohol problems in first-degree and second-degree biological relatives.

The positive feelings evoked by alcohol in individuals in the primary group lead to repeated drinking episodes, with complete disregard for the unpredictable negative consequences of alcohol use.

Among persons in the primary group, there is usually a history of inconsistency in the nurturing process when the individual was a child and adolescent, ie, loving and caring were not delivered in a consistent, dependable manner, making a "love" relationship unpredictable. Often then, a love relationship develops with alcohol, which can generate positive feelings in a predictable way. In other words, alcohol becomes a love substitute.

When one considers the genetics of alcoholism, it is probable that many persons in the primary group may, in fact, have inherited certain aspects of their disease. Recent evidence suggests that many primary "alcoholics" do not metabolize ethanol as others do and that the accumulation of certain metabolic by-products (ie, acetaldehyde) and the effect of these by-products on neurotransmitters in the central nervous system (CNS) may play a role in the early and consistent loss of control of alcohol use.

The psychopathology in these individuals is usually characterological, but with many years of heavy drinking, organic mental disorders such as organic affective syndrome or organic personality syndrome emerge as dominant processes.

Treatment implications for the primary group include establishing a goal of lifelong abstinence from alcohol and offering a consistent and predictable nurturing therapeutic process; often Alcoholics Anonymous and/or psychotherapy (group and/or individual) can be helpful.

Secondary Group

Secondary alcohol abuse/dependence occurs in persons who suffer a major psychiatric illness which preceded the onset of the destructive use of alcohol. Characteristics of the secondary "alcoholic" may include the following.

There is significant psychopathology in these individuals. Generally, the personality disorders are not considered "significant" psychopathology, with the exception of the borderline personality and schizotypal personality (DSM III). The most common psychiatric disturbance seen in the secondary group is a mood disturbance, which includes bipolar and unipolar affective disorders (manic–depressive illness), dysthymic disorders (depressive neurosis), and cyclothymic disorders. Depression and alcohol dependence have long been associated. Because heavy drinking per se can cause depression, it is important, in diagnosing the secondary "alcoholic," to establish that the drinking occurs in the midst of the depression rather than that the depression occurs in the midst of the drinking. This approach is true for other forms of significant psychopathology, which can include the anxiety disorders, the schizophrenias, somatoform disorders, and the paranoid disorders.

It is felt that these individuals use alcohol as an attempt at self-medication to ameliorate the pain and discomfort of the underlying psychopathology. Tragically, relief is only transient, and the continued and repeated use of alcohol usually exacerbates the psychopathology. The treatment implication is predicated on diagnosing both the psychiatric disturbance and the alcohol abuse/dependence and offering therapeutic intervention for both processes. It is naive to assume that successful treatment of the psychiatric problem will necessarily obviate any further difficulties with alcohol. It is in this group that rational psychopharmacotherapy can be a useful adjunct.

Persons who suffer depression secondary to chronic physical illness and disabilities and develop alcohol abuse/dependence can be classified as secondary "alcoholics."

Reactive Group

Although persons suffering primary and, to a lesser extent, secondary alcohol abuse/dependence probably constitute the largest group of "alcoholics" in treatment, it is my impression that of the millions of individuals in this country who are drinking with problems, most of these fall into the reactive group. Some characteristics of the reactive patient are: a history of successful social drinking, ie, drinking without problems; sudden or insidious development of preoccupation with alcohol after the individual experiences psychological stress perceived as overwhelming; and myriad medical and psychological complaints (subacute phase).

Among common psychosocial stresses in the reactive patient are marital separation and divorce, financial pressures, job dissatisfaction, job loss, and the existential anguish often associated with aging. Alcohol use allows the person to avoid conscious dealing with the genesis and consequence of the stressful event(s). Because all alcohol-dependent individuals can usually relate trauma in their lives, it is critical to establish by history that there was no excessive drinking prior to the psychosocial stress in order to diagnose a reactive process.

Usually individuals in the reactive group have impaired coping skills, but there is no significant disturbance in premorbid functioning and no discernible precedent psychopathology. Treatment implications involve assisting the patient to abstain from alcohol and to adopt healthier and more appropriate coping skills in dealing with past and future stressful events. It has been suggested that, with successful treatment, some of these individuals return to the use of alcohol and are able to drink without problems, and spontaneous recoveries from alcohol abuse/dependence that have been reported probably involve cases in the reactive group.

Unfortunately, the classification of alcohol-dependent persons into primary, secondary, and reactive is not always an easy process. However, if one adopts a differential diagnostic approach patterned after this model, treatment is often more flexible and specific.

Whether one is a primary, secondary, or reactive "alcoholic," the currently accepted diagnoses of alcohol abuse or dependence or of alcohol-dependence syndrome and alcohol-related disabilities can also be applied. To me it is clear, however, that this differential diagnostic approach is incompatible with the single unitary disease concept of alcoholism.

PSYCHOLOGICAL FACTORS

Although there has been a passionate search for the "alcoholic personality," there is still no agreement on whether or not such an entity exists. There are certain psychological factors, however, that occur frequently in the alcohol abusing/dependent population; recognizing and understanding these factors facilitates therapeutic intervention in the chronic phase.

Denial

Denial is the conscious and unconscious refusal to acknowledge the existence of problems and is a defense mechanism designed to guard against internal perceptions of a painful nature. Denial may assume different dimensions as suggested by the following statements:

"Doctor, I don't have a problem with alcohol; I only drink too much once in a while. Anyway, many of my friends drink more than I do."

"Doctor, I feel much better now; thank you for helping with this last drunk. I've learned my lesson, and believe me, this will never happen again. But I really don't think I need any more help now."

"Doctor, you're correct. I do have a drinking problem that is causing all of my other problems. Help me stop drinking and everything will be all right."

Denial and ambivalence toward further treatment, while certainly not specific for alcohol abuse/dependence, is very common when the patient's immediate crisis and physical comfort have been relieved.

Unfortunately, the statements: "You can't help alcoholics until they are ready to help themselves . . . " or " . . . until they hit bottom." have created an anticipatory frustration among physicians, leading to a sense of helplessness. At this juncture, it is important to recognize that most patients seeking a physician's care have a common expectation — immediate relief from psychological and/or physical pain. There is usually little initial commitment to assume personal responsibility for major life-style and behavioral changes. In other words, patients are not usually "motivated" to become partners and to participate with the physician in effecting healthy (non-illness) behaviors. Persons suffering alcohol abuse/dependence syndrome are no different. Development of the patient's internal motivation is a part of the therapeutic process and often requires that the physician apply external motivation in a firm, consistent, and ethical manner. There are a number of effective external motivating factors (coercion) which can assist the physician in overcoming the patient's denial and ambivalence.

Legal Factors

Alcohol-related charges, such as driving while intoxicated, public drunkenness, disturbing the peace, etc, represent manifest evidence of the individual's behavioral problems with alcohol. Threatened or anticipated punishment in the form of incarceration, loss of license, etc, frequently motivates (externally) a begrudging individual to enter the evaluation and treatment process. Treatment outcome is frequently very positive even though the individual was forced into therapy.

Vocational Factors

Studies have indicated that a person's job is the most important source of self-esteem and self-worth (more so than family and health). Employee assistance programs that identify the problem employee as one who cannot meet the social and vocational expectations of the job and as one whose performance is impaired secondary to alcohol abuse/dependence have traditionally enjoyed significant success in returning these persons to work after treatment has been initiated. The critical factor appears to be the humane and non-judgmental use of external motivation, ie, job jeopardy. Whenever possible and feasible, the physician, with the patient's permission, should establish a relationship with the employer within the ethical and legal guidelines of confidentiality. However, even without establishing a liaison with the employer, the physician can utilize the anticipated loss of employment in therapy as an inducement for compliance.

Family Factors

Alcohol abuse/dependence affects all members of the family and leads to disruption and deterioration of relationships within both the nuclear and extended families. Affected family members not only develop feelings of anger, resentment, and guilt, but these same persons often consciously and unconsciously become enablers for the alcohol-dependent member. Enabling is a process of making social and job excuses and assuming responsibilities that have previously been relegated to the patient. Whenever possible, family members should be involved in the initial phase of evaluation and treatment. Immediate goals of this involvement include: (a) support in ameliorating feelings of anger, resentment, and guilt; (b) assistance to family members in establishing tolerance limits on the patient's alcohol-related behaviors; (c) recognition that precipitation of a family crisis often externally motivates that patient to enter and remain in treatment; (d) exploration of various options open especially to the spouse but also to other family members such as dissolution of the relationship v continued involvement in the day-to-day drama of the disease, ie, development of a separate and meaningful life (career, etc); (e) help to family members in avoiding idle threats when no true intent exists; and (f) the changing of enabling behaviors which involve excuse-making and alternately rescuing and persecuting the patient. Referral to Al-Anon and Alateen can be invaluable assistance to the treating physician in the effective integration of family members into the treatment process.

Health Factors

It is well recognized that patients are seldom frightened away from drinking strictly on the basis of the tissue toxicity of alcohol. Telling a patient that he or she will soon die from cirrhosis unless drinking ceases is an empty admonition and seldom occurs as predicted; such an admonition only serves to generate continuing doubt concerning the skills of the treating physician and, indeed, of physicians in general. However, the possibility and reality of alcohol-induced physical illness can have a motivating influence, particularly in encouraging the patient to enter the initial phase of treatment. Health factors are more significant when alcohol abuse/dependence is diagnosed in the earlier stages. As concerns denial and motivation, the physician should recognize that "externally" motivating patients in an ethical way is a key factor in the success of treatment outcome. The physician must recognize that: (a) the patient's ambivalence toward further treatment when physical improvement has occurred is an integral part of the disease(s); (b) early involvement of significant others in the patient's life, such as spouse, children, employer, friends, in the external motivating process is extremely important; (c) most patients have their own "bottom" or "moment of truth," a psychosocial level that can often be externally precipitated; and (d) the appropriate and ethical use of rational authority (external motivation, coercion) by the physician is not only a valid approach, but frequently is necessary to initiate early treatment and insure a long-term commitment to the principles of treatment.

Depression

Recent advances in biological psychiatry have prompted a more creative and clinically pragmatic nosological approach to affective (mood) disorders, particularly depression. With these advances, the clinical impression that alcohol abuse/dependence and depression are closely associated has been confirmed. It is exceedingly important from both a therapeutic and prognostic viewpoint to determine whether or not the alcohol dependence and the depression are primary or secondary processes.

Knowledge of the changes in CNS neurotransmitter activity (ie, noradrenalin and serotonin) in depressed patients provides a speculative basis for explaining why persons who drink heavily become depressed. Alcohol directly and indirectly adversely affects the ATPase system in cell membranes of the CNS. As a result, Na^+ accumulates intracellularly and decreases the synaptic availability of and/or the postsynaptic sensitivity to norepinephrine (and possibly serotonin). These changes have been associated with the clinical state of depression. When this process is caused by alcohol, the biochemical lesion is considered to be reversible, and with abstinence from alcohol for 30 days, the depressed mood usually diminishes. History in these patients must clearly establish that the depression occurs in the midst of heavy drinking and thus is secondary to ethyl alcohol. It is generally felt that alcohol-induced depression should not be treated with antidepressants; however, if significant depression is sustained beyond 30 days of abstinence, other diagnostic considerations must be entertained.

Many studies have indicated that among the causes of secondary alcohol abuse/dependence, an affective illness is one of the most frequent underlying psychiatric disorders. With a unipolar affective illness (major depression), the patient cyclicly exhibits mood changes from euthymia to depression. With a bipolar affective illness, the patient cyclicly exhibits mood changes from mania–hypomania to euthymia to depression. In addition, patients with unipolar and bipolar disorders often have a positive family history of affective illness. With a dysthymic disorder (depressive neurosis) the patient's symptoms of depression do not meet criteria for a major depression but are severe enough to cause considerable dysfunction. It is necessary to establish that episodes of mood changes occurred prior to any major life problem caused by alcohol and that they occur in the absence of heavy alcohol use, drug abuse, or as a consequence of any other psychiatric disorder (ie, the schizophrenias). More frequently, secondary alcohol abuse/dependence will occur in the midst of mood changes (usually depression); because of the action of alcohol on the CNS, the underlying depression will be exacerbated and prolonged. It is in these patients that rational psychopharmacotherapy (ie, antidepressants, lithium) may be necessary. As stated previously, treatment must address both the psychiatric disorder (affective illness) and the alcohol abuse/dependence.

The following paradigm demonstrates the complicating and exacerbating influence exerted by alcohol use in those persons suffering an affective illness.

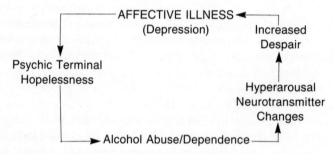

In my experience, there appears to be a subgroup of depressive alcoholics with the following characteristics:

- Ten- to 15-year history of heavy (episodic or continuous alcohol abuse/ dependence) usually preceded by years of drinking without problems.
- Depressive episodes that did not initially precede alcohol dependence but that increase in severity with age and chronicity of alcohol use.
- An emergent pattern of mood lability (euthymia→depression) without precipitating causes or disproportionate in severity with apparent precipitating causes.
- Loss of control of alcohol use similar to that seen in persons suffering from primary alcohol dependence. However, loss of control occurs only after years of heavy drinking.
- Alcohol use coincides with the onset of depression.
- Clinical picture of a unipolar affective illness, with a negative family history of depression and/or alcohol dependence.

It is possible that in these individuals the long-term effects of alcohol on the neurotransmitters as described are such that previous reversibility of abnormalities in biogenic amine metabolism is compromised. In other words, it is possible that alcohol has caused an "acquired" unipolar affective illness. The response of such individuals to psychopharmacotherapy has not yet been elucidated.

Recognizing that there is a close association between depression and alcohol abuse/dependence, the physician, by rigorously applying the DMS-III diagnostic criteria for affective disorders, can usually discern the presence of primary depression and secondary alcohol problems or of primary alcohol dependence and secondary depression. This differentiation is essential in formulating a meaningful treatment approach.

Dependency

Prior to the onset of alcohol abuse/dependence, the history usually reveals significant difficulties in interpersonal relationships in regard to dependency needs and the manner in which these needs are satisfied. From the standpoint of treatment, Blane's division of specific clinical typologies based on dependent behaviors at the interpersonal level is useful. These typologies include the dependent patient, the counterdependent patient and the dependent–independent patient.[3]

The Dependent Patient

The following psychological paradigm summarizes the process of the dependent patient.

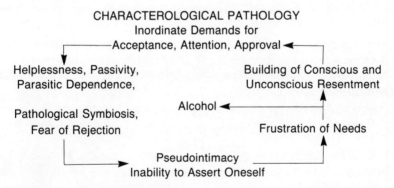

CHARACTEROLOGICAL PATHOLOGY
Inordinate Demands for
Acceptance, Attention, Approval

Helplessness, Passivity,
Parasitic Dependence,

Building of Conscious and
Unconscious Resentment

Pathological Symbiosis,
Fear of Rejection

Alcohol

Frustration of Needs

Pseudointimacy
Inability to Assert Oneself

This pattern is seen more frequently in women; however, men are certainly not excluded. The person enters adulthood with inordinate demands for acceptance, approval, and attention. Frequently, he or she is a product of either emotional and social deprivation during childhood and adolescence, or of overindulgence ("spoiled"), and functions under the assumption that "Everyone has to like me"; there is an almost disabling fear of rejection. The person enters interpersonal relationships in a very helpless, passive manner, frequently presenting with the "doormat syndrome," ie, "Everyone is always taking advantage of me." The relationships are pseudointimate; the person is unable to externalize anger in an appropriately assertive fashion, largely from fear of rejection. Frustration, occurring because needs for approval, attention, and acceptance are not being met, leads to the development of conscious and unconscious resentment and anger, which are largely self-directed. The cycle becomes vicious.

Often these persons begin using alcohol as a "people" substitute; in essence, "the bottle" becomes a good friend; the dependency on alcohol is without the attendant risks of intimacy and rejection that accompany "people" relationships.

The behavioral reaction to alcohol is of the "Jekyll and Hyde" variety. These people are described as follows. "She's (he's) the sweetest, nicest person in the world until she (he) drinks; then she (he) becomes hostile, aggressive, and angry for no apparent reason." If the diagnosis of alcohol abuse/dependence is made, these patients will at first interact with the physician in the initial phase of treatment in a very seductive way. A typical statement is "Doctor Knott, I have a serious drinking problem. I've heard of your reputation, and if anyone can help me, you can. I'm completely in your hands. Doctor, cure me." (When I first entered the alcoholism field, I used to believe such a statement.) The patient is entering the therapeutic relationship in the same helpless, dependent way that is characteristic of his or her other interpersonal relationships. Although ego-inflating, the physician should avoid being trapped with such seduction. One of the foundations in the psychotherapeutic management of such patients is assertiveness training.

The Counterdependent Patient

The following psychological paradigm describes the process of the counterdependent patient.

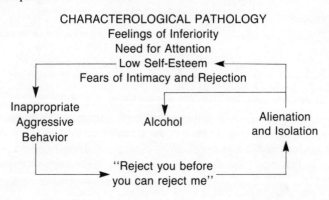

CHARACTEROLOGICAL PATHOLOGY
Feelings of Inferiority
Need for Attention
Low Self-Esteem
Fears of Intimacy and Rejection

Inappropriate Aggressive Behavior

Alcohol

Alienation and Isolation

"Reject you before you can reject me"

This description applies to men more than women; however, the latter are certainly not excluded. Again, these persons enter adulthood with inordinate needs for attention, feelings of inferiority, and fears of intimacy and rejection. Emotional and social deprivation or overindulgence during childhood and adolescence are also frequent precedents to this type of characterological pathology. But instead of structuring interpersonal relationships in a helpless, passive way, these persons are inappropriately aggressive (both sober and intoxicated) and deal with other individuals with the attitude: "I'm going to reject you before you can reject me. I'll not allow anyone to get close to me because eventually I'll be rejected." There is consequently significant alienation and isolation at the interpersonal level and the person frequently turns to alcohol as a "people" substitute, decreasing the risks of intimacy and rejection. Further, with these patients, it is very difficult initially to establish a warm and effective therapeutic relationship, since the physician's initial contact is often characterized by the following encounter: "Dr Knott, you've suggested that I have a drinking problem. Well, I've heard of your reputation, and let me tell you this — even if I did have a drinking problem, you couldn't help. I never want to see you again."

If the physician can tolerate the "I'll reject you before you can reject me" approach of the patient and develop a therapeutic relationship, further psychotherapy has a chance of being successful.

The Dependent–Independent Patient

Although the previous descriptions of dependent behaviors represent rather clear-cut processes, frequently such behaviors are manifest as an admixture and change with time. The following psychological paradigm describes the process of the dependent–independent patient.

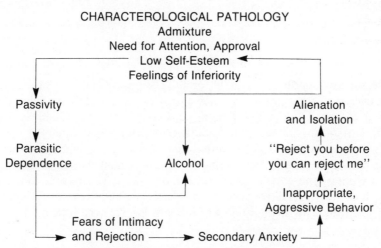

CHARACTEROLOGICAL PATHOLOGY
Admixture
Need for Attention, Approval
Low Self-Esteem
Feelings of Inferiority

Passivity

Parasitic
Dependence

Alcohol

Alienation
and Isolation

"Reject you before
you can reject me"

Inappropriate,
Aggressive Behavior

Fears of Intimacy
and Rejection ——→ Secondary Anxiety

These categories of dependent behaviors are presented as thematic processes in many patients who suffer alcohol abuse/dependence and not as absolute typologies into which all patients must fit. Understanding the dynamics is more useful to the physician than is reliance on terms such as passive-dependent or passive-aggressive personality disorders alone.

Narcissism

Although most persons harbor some narcissistic traits, there are those whose fantasies in this regard lead to marked social and psychological dysfunction. The following paradigm characterizes these individuals.

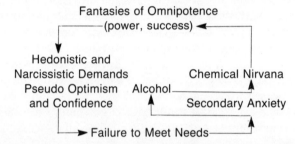

This characterological disorder probably affects alcohol-abusing/-dependent men more than women. This person, usually a product of a dominating mother and/or spouse, has a need to present himself as invulnerable and irresistible to women. Fantasies and needs involve unlimited success, social and personal power, and sexual prowess. Failure to meet these needs at the interpersonal level creates secondary anxieties. Alcohol is a particularly dangerous yet seductive drug for such persons because it releases inhibitions and pharmacologically creates a "chemical nirvana," ie, alcohol reinforces the fantasies.

PSYCHOTHERAPY

When faced with the opportunity for and responsibility of psychotherapy, many nonpsychiatrist physicians have a tendency to avoid the psychotherapeutic encounter by either ignoring the need or referring the individual. This is especially true with the alcohol-abusing/-dependent patient.

It is common for treatment failures to be ascribed to a lack of motivation on the part of the patient; frequently, the therapist's contribution to the treatment failure is ignored. The phenomenon of countertransference as a process that can either facilitate or obstruct effective psychotherapeutic intervention in patients with alcohol-related problems has received little attention.[4]

Countertransference can be defined as "the total emotional reaction of the therapist to the patient, with consideration of the wide range of conscious, preconscious and unconscious attitudes, beliefs and feelings in the therapist" who comes in contact with the patient with alcohol problems. The frequent feelings of fear, anger, rage, negativism, hopelessness, and helplessness experienced by the physician-therapist when dealing with these patients result from the countertransferential process.

Although the clinician may intellectually embrace the therapeutic virtues of empathy and understanding, actual therapeutic behaviors are often structured by countertransferential mechanisms that actually obstruct effective intervention. Some of the more common forms of these mechanisms are listed below.[4]

1. The therapist who has a need to be all-loving and all-giving frequently assumes the role of the "good parent rescuing the bad, impulsive child." The clinical behaviors are characterized as being overinvolved, overly permissive, and overprotective. The patient will initially accept such overtures from the therapist and then regress and act out in a negativistic, noncompliant manner. The therapist, perceiving betrayal, feels angry and hurt; the patient is viewed as resistant and untreatable and is either discharged from or referred elsewhere for treatment.

2. The perceived omnipotence of the physician-therapist is frequently the target of the patient who will manipulate for prescription medication. The physician who is unaware of his or her prescribing practices is vulnerable to such manipulation because it perpetuates the sense of omnipotence. On the other hand, the patient views the process as a "scam." This therapeutic game frequently allows iatrogenicity to sustain the alcohol/drug dependence problem.

3. The therapist whose needs dictate complete control of the therapeutic alliance will be gratified by the early and remarkable improvement that many patients achieve. As the therapist begins to bask in the self-imposed "glory" of the effectiveness of treatment, the patient will regress, act out, and become noncompliant. The clinician then will become depressed, angry, and guilty about being a "bad therapist." The therapeutic alliance should be based on sharing, not assuming the responsibility for the patient's recovery.

4. The therapist often overidentifies with the patient's behaviors and assumes the posture of "you and me against the world." This may result from many unconscious impulse fantasies of the therapist which are fulfilled through the acting-out behaviors of the patient. Such an approach is often perceived by the patient as approval of such behaviors, and an enabling rather than therapeutic process prevails.

5. The therapist suffering from "burnout" may be unaware of the countertransferential consequences such as indifference, boredom, emotional distancing, and a separation from therapeutic interaction.

The American Medical Association's definition (as modified by Blanc) of psychotherapy is very useful in regard to the treatment of patients with alcohol-related problems.[3]

> Psychotherapy is a structured, emotional experience occurring in a close relationship between two or more persons in which a trained individual helps another to achieve greater self-understanding, objectivity and personal growth through a series of contacts in which relevant inner experiences and life situations of the latter are discussed.

This definition can apply to both individual and group psychotherapy. The following discussion focuses primarily on individual psychotherapy involving the physician–patient relationship.

Realistically, most physicians practice psychotherapy as defined above with their patients. This definition is especially pertinent for alcohol-abusing/ -dependent patients since it makes no assumptions about the single unitary disease concept of alcoholism yet recognizes that psychological and emotional problems are present and can be effectively managed with various psychotherapeutic techniques. Generally, psychotherapy needs to be predicated on the assumption that no two patients are exactly the same; flexibility and versatility are the hallmarks of an effective approach.

There are four major areas to be discussed: (a) factors that may have caused the alcohol problem; (b) factors that are caused by the alcohol problem, (c) factors that occur with abstinence from alcohol, and (d) factors involved with relapses.[3]

As the physician initiates psychotherapy, it is essential to recognize that the personalities of both therapist and patient determine the nature of the structured relationship; the influence of these personalities is generally more important than the specific approach which is chosen.

Factors that May Have Caused the Alcohol Abuse/Dependence Problem

The division of the factors that may have caused the alcohol abuse/dependence problem into proximal and distal is very useful in the psychotherapeutic process. Proximal factors involve events which appear to precipitate drinking episodes. Usually these involve interpersonal conflicts stemming from dependent, counterdependent, or dependent–independent behaviors. Distal factors involve difficulties during childhood and adolescent development, primarily interaction with parents, and with other adult role models and peers, with emphasis on the presence or absence of and the consistency or inconsistency of the nurturing process. Understanding the critical distal factors will permit both the physician-therapist and the patient better interpretation of the reaction to proximal factors which lead to the destructive use of alcohol.

Patients should begin to understand, from a mutual exploration of their responses to immediate problems, something of a personal psychodynamics and maladaptive reactions involved.[5] The physician should try to elicit the subjective meaning that patients have given to the stressful events. For example:

- Who or what is producing angry feelings?
- What does loss or threat mean to the patient and his life?
- What is the cause of the patient's ambivalent feelings?
- What role have the patient's reactions played in the excessive drinking pattern and how will this affect recovery?
- What are some different ways of coping with these kinds of stress?

Alcohol abuse/dependence frequently leads to medical, psychological, social, and legal difficulties. Dealing with and, whenever possible, assisting the patient in the resolution of these difficulties, usually through crisis intervention, is important to the patient's successful entry into and continuation with psychotherapy. In essence, this rescuing process should only be a component of long-term rehabilitation. The management of life crises, while necessary, should not replace or dilute efforts toward enhancing self-understanding and personal growth. The physician should not assume total responsibility for crisis intervention; utilization of other resources, ie, social workers, clergymen, Alcoholics Anonymous, psychologists, etc, is frequently necessary.

Factors that Occur with Abstinence

Alcohol is frequently a "people" substitute for patients; removal of this substitute is perceived by the patient as a major object loss. The patient should be allowed and even encouraged to "mourn" this loss, that is, to experience a grief reaction as with any other object loss.

Other factors emerge during abstinence from alcohol that represent certain dangers to the patient. By identifying these early in psychotherapy, the physician can prepare the patient to deal with them on a more realistic basis. By predicting these dangers, the physician only strengthens the therapeutic relationship. The patient will frequently, either implicitly or explicitly, respond by saying, "Doctor, you told me this was going to happen; you must know what you're talking about." Some common problems may face the patient during the abstinent period.[1]

The "honeymoon" period. If patients achieve effective abstinence from alcohol early in treatment, they will most likely receive positive reinforcement from family, friends, employer, etc, for the behavioral change. This will continue for a few weeks and possibly for two to three months. Then, gradually, the significant others in a patient's life will begin to take the behavioral change for granted and indeed expect it rather than hope for it. As positive reinforcement decreases, patients may interpret this as lack of support or even overt rejection. A return to the use of alcohol occurs frequently at this time. If the patient can anticipate this, and if therapy can be directed toward development of an internal rather than external system of reinforcement by the patient, the sense of vulnerability can be markedly attenuated.

The problem of sexual dysfunction. The abstinent alcoholic, particularly a man, should be prepared for the possibility of some sexual dysfunction early in treatment. If this is not discussed, the patient frequently feels as if he is impotent or as if she is frigid and is often extremely reluctant to broach the subject in therapy situations. The problem is usually not one of impotence but rather a decrease in libidinal drive consequent to the removal of alcohol, which had previously caused a sexually disinhibiting effect and thus an augmented libido. Reassuring the patient and talking with the patient and mate jointly or separately concerning seeking alternative methods for libidinal stimulation will decrease anxiety and prevent the patient from feeling emasculated or frigid.

The problem of trust versus mistrust. With the dramatic change in behavior that can occur early in treatment, the patient often seeks not only positive reinforcement from significant others, but also complete trust from others that the new behavior will continue indefinitely. It is important to point out to the patient that the spouse and/or employer and/or friends may view this change with some initial skepticism, and some element of mistrust should be expected. Emphasizing the destructive effect that the drinking behavior has had in the past on interpersonal relationships encourages the patient to be more realistic in what can be expected immediately from these relationships.

The problem of dysphoria associated with an increased awareness. Many patients imagine that with abstinence from alcohol, symptoms of anxiety and depression that normally result from situational stress will no longer occur. In fact, anxiety-depressive symptomatology may be perceived more acutely by the patient without the chemical camouflage of alcohol. Prediction of this by the physician will ameliorate the pain and frustration that characterize the initial phase of treatment.

Factors Associated with Relapses

At the beginning of therapy, it is imperative that the physician clearly define responsibility for drinking-abstinence issues by stating to the patient: "It is not my responsibility to stop your drinking, nor is it my responsibility if you return to drinking; that is your responsibility." A relapse usually involves other illness behaviors besides alcohol use which either precede and/or occur comcomitantly with drinking. Precedent illness behaviors are often a harbinger to such a relapse. Recidivistic drinking often signifies a testing of the therapeutic relationship, with the patient's asking, "If I drink again, will treatment be terminated?" In addition, drinking sometimes represents anger and hostility toward the physician if the patient becomes disappointed with the therapeutic process. The physician can expect relapses as part of the disease trajectory in 50% to 60% of alcohol-abusing/-dependent patients, but this expectation should not be conveyed to the patient. Recognizing that abstinence is a means to an end and is not the *sine qua non* of recovery, the physician can assist the patient toward a better understanding of proximal and distal factors involved with repeated alcohol use. Frequently, a relapse offers the opportunity to discover new insights and may necessitate a change in the therapeutic approach. The patient should understand that a relapse does not necessarily mean the termination of treatment but rather a phase of recovery that should be further explored and resolved within the structure of the therapeutic relationships.

Within the context of the previous discussion, addressing certain critical issues has been useful to me in dealing with the alcohol-abusing/-dependent patient from a psychotherapeutic point of view. Among these issues are: (a) flexibility and versatility; (b) emotional support; (c) practical support; (d) emotional reeducation; (e) abstinence *v* drinking during treatment; (f) responsibility for recovery; (g) behavioral approach to treatment; and (h) recovery *v* control.

Flexibility and Versatility

The disease trajectory of alcohol abuse/dependence is similar to that of other chronic illnesses and is represented by the following diagram.

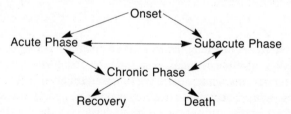

The disease trajectory is a multidirectional, dynamic process. Intervention with the different phases and with the process itself demands an eclectic flexibility and versatility, utilizing not only the diagnostic and treatment skills of the physician, but those of persons from other disciplines as well.

Emotional Support

The most important aspect of any therapy is the patient's relationship with the therapist. It is important for patients to feel understood and to believe that with the therapist's help they can begin to manage their lives again. Understanding a patient involves gaining knowledge of the family history, of the development of attitudes and reactions in childhood and adolescence, of the problems encountered in day-to-day living, and of the situational factors and stress that may precipitate alcohol ingestion. It is important to realize that the patient's problems and discomforts are subjectively perceived and felt, regardless of how the therapist interprets the situation. Support should be offered in a nonmoralistic, nonjudgmental way.

Practical Support

Intellectual insight into problems and possible solutions is not tantamount to recovery. Patients must not only learn effective problem-solving techniques, but must also be encouraged to put them into action. The consequence of behavioral change may be more painful than remaining in a "familiar hell." Practical support involves defining alternative coping mechanisms from a behavioral point of view and insisting that patients be responsible for the choice of these alternatives.

Emotional Reeducation

Quite often, anxious-depressed alcohol-abusing/-dependent patients have developed defenses that protect them from admitting the extent of their problems with alcohol. It is important to be aware of and to deal with any internal or external factors in a patient's life that maintain the status quo and resist change.

Abstinence Versus Drinking During Treatment

Various attitudes concerning the issue of abstinence v drinking during treatment for alcohol abuse/dependence include the belief that the patient must achieve abstinence as soon as possible and maintain abstinence during treatment, or must achieve abstinence as soon as possible and maintain abstinence not only during treatment, but on a lifelong basis. On the contrary, another belief is that the patient will probably continue drinking during treatment, and, if alcohol use is not obstructing treatment, it will diminish and (it is hoped) disappear if therapy is successful.

In my experience, abstinence should be achieved as soon as possible and should be maintained during treatment. Lifelong abstinence is essential for recovery from primary alcohol dependence. Many patients attempt "controlled" alcohol use on their own during or after treatment. Although a few secondary alcoholics and reactive alcoholics allegedly return to a level of alcohol use without problems, this is an extremely dangerous treatment goal to establish. Increased attention is being paid to the issue of controlled drinking as a therapeutic goal. To date, the limited research in this area is contradictory and has resulted in a great deal of inflammatory rhetoric. Until (if ever) specific criteria can be established as to who might or might not be able to resume alcohol use safely, the best course is one of abstinence.

Responsibility for Recovery

In the beginning of treatment and throughout treatment, the physician must emphasize that he or she is a facilitator in the recovery process, but that the patient is personally responsible for healthy v illness behaviors. A rational therapy approach is necessary. One must say to the patient, "Your illness (irresponsible) behaviors occur not because you are sick; rather, your sickness exists because of your illness (irresponsible) behaviors." The alcohol-abusing/ -dependent patient who erroneously accepts the identity of an "alcoholic" as being weak, passive, dependent, inadequate, self-centered, etc, will often achieve sobriety but will continue to engage in illness behaviors, saying, "I'm an alcoholic, and you know how alcoholics are." Continuing to emphasize the patient's personal responsibility for recovery will permit the physician to be a facilitator and a partner in health rather than be manipulated into assuming the dominant role in the process of and recovery from the patient's disease.

Behavioral Approach to Treatment

Most experienced clinicians in the field of alcohology recognize the behavioral aspects of alcohol abuse/dependence. Behavioral modification involving alcohol use (and other illness behaviors) is generally considered to be one of the cornerstones of treatment and can legitimately be classified as a component of psychotherapy as previously defined. Behavioral modification techniques that have enjoyed some success include: relaxation training (muscle relaxation training, systematic desensitization, biofeedback, transcendental meditation); assertiveness training; and relationship counseling. In regard to the latter, the use of behavioral contracts, with well-defined, realistic, measurable goals and objectives, is very helpful. Such contracts can be developed between the physician and patient and between the patient and significant others (family, friends, employer). Behavioral approaches are attempts to use external methods of control as a means of teaching the patient more appropriate internal methods of control.

Behavioral changes, including abstinence from alcohol, are necessary precedents and concomitants to continuing effective psychotherapy. All too frequently, the patient states, "I'll change my behaviors as soon as my feelings and attitudes change." The physician's response should be, "No, you must begin changing behaviors and then we'll deal with the associated feelings and attitudes."

Recovery Versus Control

The following definition of alcoholism (Mann, 1958) has been widely accepted and is pertinent to the issue of recovery or control.

Alcoholism is a disease which manifests itself chiefly by the uncontrollable drinking of the victim, who is known as an alcoholic. It is a progressive disease, which, if left untreated, grows more virulent year by year, driving its victims further and further from the normal world, and deeper and deeper into an abyss which has only two outlets: insanity or death. Alcoholism, therefore, is a progressive and often fatal disease . . . if it is not treated and arrested. But it can be arrested.

This definition implies that the best that can be hoped for is arrest of the disease and that there is a continuing effort to control the disease, a concept somewhat antithetical to the idea of recovery. However, since 1958, a number of factors have emerged which suggest that such a definition may be too restrictive and does not necessarily apply to all patients. There have been reports of spontaneous recovery from "alcoholism" without treatment, and reports of "alcoholics" who return to a safe level of drinking. In addition, there is now recognition that many different types of alcoholism (primary, secondary, and reactive) may exist. Finally, the success of treatment outcome may depend more on the number of treatment contacts than on the specific types of treatment offered.

The goal of treatment is to assist the patient to achieve a level of functioning that does not involve an alcohol-centered existence. The fear that the arrest-control process will be a lifelong struggle prevents many patients from entering or continuing with treatment. To argue about control *v* recovery is counterproductive. Much more beneficial for the patient is the physician's orientation, one that signifies to the patient: "You have a disease; that disease is treatable. You can expect to improve dramatically. Alcohol is not necessary to your existence or the quality of your life."

CHEMOTHERAPY

Psychopharmacotherapy

There have been widely divergent and extreme positions concerning the use of psychoactive drugs in the alcohol-abusing/-dependent patient. One school of thought states emphatically that the alcoholic has an addictive personality, and that the use of any mind-altering drug is dangerous and to be avoided totally. Another school seriously asserts that humans have always and will always be chemically oriented in regard to the pharmacological manipulation of feelings, and therefore a more realistic approach would be to supply a drug that is less harmful than alcohol (ie, the experimental use of marijuana as a replacement for alcohol). Both of these views can be therapeutically nihilistic.

Invariably, the detoxified patient (primary, secondary, or reactive) complains of anxiety and depression. In most but not all cases, the anxiety is secondary to the depression. In selected cases, when these symptoms produce significant dysfunction, the administration of a psychoactive drug may be an effective adjunct. For primary anxiety states, the use of antihistamines (hydroxyzine, diphenhydramine) is effective. Extreme caution must be taken when sedative-hypnotics are prescribed (ie, benzodiazepines) because of the potential for cross-dependence and dual dependence. Many physicians feel strongly that sedative-hypnotics should be confined to the detoxification period only.

When symptoms of depression (after detoxification) are sufficiently serious to mandate chemotherapy, proper selection of an antidepressant (tricyclic, monoamine oxidase [MAO] inhibitor) can be helpful in the initial phase of therapy. Criteria for a bona fide affective illness should be met before antidepressant agents are used. The use of lithium should be reserved for those patients suffering from a unipolar or bipolar affective illness. There are insufficient data to suggest that alcohol abuse/dependence per se is an indication for empirical lithium therapy. It is obvious that major psychiatric disorders that occur with secondary alcohol abuse/dependence can often benefit from the appropriate use of psychopharmacological agents.

According to the tenets of rational psychopharmacotherapy, the patient should understand that no drug can replace alcohol in regard to rapidity of action and initial euphoria; that the drug being prescribed is for a specific purpose, ie, to ameliorate or remove symptoms of an underlying psychiatric problem; and that drug therapy is only adjunctive — alone, it is insufficient to produce effective recovery.

Antidisatropics

From its early use as an antioxidant in the rubber industry through clinical trials as an antihelminthic, disulfiram (Antabuse) emerged serendipitously more than forty years ago as a drug initially hailed as the "cure for alcoholism."

By interfering with the normal metabolic breakdown of ethanol, disulfiram in combination with alcohol produces a disulfiram–ethanol reaction (DER) that is physiologically uncomfortable.

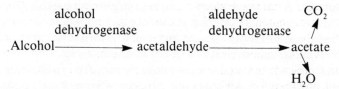

Disulfiram inhibits aldehyde dehydrogenase, thus preventing the breakdown of acetaldehyde, which, because of its toxicity, is otherwise metabolized very rapidly. Elevated acetaldehyde levels, as a result of the DER, result in signs and symptoms such as: flushed facies, "tightness" in the chest, headaches, diaphoresis, nausea, vomiting, and orthostatic hypotension. This reaction can occur with the ingestion of as little as 2 oz of wine or 3 to 4 oz of beer. If Antabuse is taken and alcohol subsequently is ingested, the onset of the DER usually occurs in 15 to 20 minutes; duration is from one to several hours. Patients describe the reaction as having a "bad case of the flu." Usually, the DER is mild and self-limiting; in many cases, treatment is unnecessary. In those patients requiring pharmacological amelioration of the symptoms of DER, intramuscular (IM) antihistamines (Benadryl) and Vitamin C rapidly reverse the reaction.

Disulfiram, as is true with any other drug, produces certain side effects which, in the case of this drug, have been exaggerated. The most frequent side effect is sedation; this usually responds to a dosage reduction. Sedation can be a positive side effect, particularly when used on an h.s. basis. Other less frequent side effects include a metallic taste, a garlic-like odor to breath and sweat, symptoms of "indigestion," and rarely dermatitis medicamentosa, peripheral neuritis, and decreased sexual potency. There are, however, other rare but potentially severe psychiatric side effects. Because of these, I feel strongly that disulfiram should be prescribed and monitored by physicians only.

Disulfiram affects enzyme systems other than the aldehyde dehydrogenase.

$$\text{Disulfiram} \xrightarrow{\text{Hepatic}} \text{diethyldithiocarbamate (DDC)}$$

Diethyldithiocarbamate also inhibits dopamine B hydroxylase.

$$\text{DOPA} \rightarrow \text{Dopamine} \xrightarrow{\text{dopamine B hydroxylase}} \text{Norepinephrine}$$

This action may explain the two major psychiatric side effects which, although rare, can certainly compromise treatment. The first is depression, which develops over the course of many months of disulfiram therapy. Differential diagnosis is difficult but possible through careful history-taking and skillful monitoring of the patient. If disulfiram-induced, the depression clears rapidly with discontinuation of disulfiram.

Emergence of psychotic symptoms is a more serious psychiatric side effect. There are two ways in which patients can become psychotic secondary to disulfiram. First, in patients suffering secondary alcohol abuse/dependence in whom there is an underlying major psychiatric disorder (schizophrenia, affective disorders), the removal of alcohol as a self-medicant allows the psychiatric disturbance to become more clinically manifest. In these cases, it is not the disulfiram per se but instead the absence of alcohol that is etiological. Psychotic symptoms usually become evident after a number of weeks or months of disulfiram therapy.

On the other hand, a rare patient will exhibit signs of a toxic psychosis characterized by hallucinations, paranoid delusions, disorientation, and even delirium. Onset is explosive, usually occurring within a few days to two weeks after initiation of disulfiram, and promptly subsides with discontinuation of the drug. It is not possible to predict which patients will develop a toxic psychosis.

Administration of disulfiram is absolutely contraindicated for: (a) the severely depressed suicidal patient; (b) the patient who cannot understand the effects and side effects of the drug; (c) the patient who is truly hypersensitive to the drug; and (d) patients with unstable angina or a recent myocardial infarction. Relative contraindications include patients with advanced cardiovascular, hepatic, or renal disease who may not be able physiologically to tolerate a DER.

When prescribing disulfiram for a patient, the physician should be aware of potential drug interactions. Although the concomitant use of disulfiram and dilantin, coumadin, oral hypoglycemics, isoniazid, and Flagyl is not absolutely contraindicated, CNS side effects (confusion, ataxia, disorientation) can occur; knowledge of potential drug interaction and frequent evaluation of the patient are necessary. One must assess the benefit of abstinence from alcohol v possible drug interactions when managing these patients.

Although disulfiram, when first introduced, was prescribed in daily doses of 4,000 mg, it has become apparent that a dose of 250 mg daily (usually h.s.) is sufficient to offer protection.

The success of disulfiram therapy is directly dependent on the confidence which the prescribing physician has in the drug and the enthusiasm with which it is being presented to the patient. One must ask oneself four basic questions when contemplating administration of disfulfiram. Does the patient thoroughly understand the rationale of Antabuse therapy? Are there any contraindications to Antabuse (eg, hypersensitivity, concomitant psychosis, severe organic brain syndrome, strong suicidal potential)? What is the apparent level of the patient's motivation? Does the patient understand that abstinence is a means to an end (recovery), and that its use is only adjunctive in the overall treatment process?

By emphasizing the use of Antabuse as an "insurance policy" rather than a "crutch" and stressing that a period of abstinence will allow the patient to make essential behavioral and attitudinal changes more easily, the physician adopts a positive approach to Antabuse therapy. This positive approach, emphasizing behavioral changes possible with abstinence, is frequently incorporated by the patient.

Seven major clinical indications for disulfiram therapy, as outlined by Gitlow,[6] are:

1. For early evaluation of the patient's commitment to abstinence from alcohol as being necessary for and fundamental to treatment.

2. For use in persons who must remain abstinent because of legal difficulties, ie, probation and parole. As Gitlow has observed, and as I have also found, "enforced" abstinence may well facilitate recovery from alcohol abuse/dependence.
3. As external control for the impulsive drinker.
4. As relief from preoccupation with drinking in the person who may be sober but who ruminates and struggles constantly about whether or not to have a "couple of drinks."
5. As temporary protection for persons who have achieved effective abstinence but who are suffering a life crisis, such as job loss, divorce, separation, or death of a significant other.
6. As an adjunct to the patient who, despite apparent compliance with a psychotherapeutic program, is unable to make any significant gains because of continued drinking or frequent relapses.
7. As relief for the anxieties and mistrust of significant others (such as spouse or employer) in regard to the patient's achieving and maintaining abstinence.

The manner in which disulfiram therapy is presented to the patient by the physician is critical to the success of this treatment modality. After disulfiram therapy and its rationale are explained by the physician, the patient may reply, "I don't want to take it because it's a crutch, and I can do it on my own." I frequently use the following example. "We've established the goal of abstinence for you. But let's discuss another goal, which is for you to reach the top of a five-story building. You can do this in one of two ways—either take the elevator or scale the building with a rope. Which do you choose?" The patient invariably responds, "I'll take the elevator; it's a lot easier." I respond, "Disulfiram and the elevator are very similar. Disulfiram will make it easier for you to achieve and maintain abstinence and will certainly make therapy more effective." Often the patient will see the logic of this and comply with treatment. If a patient steadfastly refuses to take disulfiram, often using illogical reasoning, the situation becomes clear. The response to a patient who states, "I don't intend to drink," is, "Although you may not intend to drink, you want the option to drink if the pressure becomes too great." The patient generally acknowledges this; frequently, effective therapy can begin whether or not the patient takes disulfiram. The length of time of disulfiram therapy should be individualized and can vary from six months to two years or longer. Although considerable controversy still surrounds the efficacy of this drug, in my experience, it can be an extremely useful adjunct when combined with other therapeutic modalities.

REFERRAL

Management of the patient in the chronic phase is a responsibility that should be shared rather than assumed solely by the physician. The complexity of the psychosocial and medical problems of these patients requires an individualized treatment plan that includes other resources. However, the physician can effectively orchestrate this plan and can appropriately guide and direct the patient into and through a treatment system.

Patients who anticipate or who, in the past, have experienced rejection from other therapeutic resources must be assured of the physician's knowledge, skill, support, interest, and availability as a critical member of the treatment team. Referral of patients should be made in a positive manner and should be based on specific needs rather than represent a negative mechanism for ignoring or rejecting the individual. In exercising referral options, careful consideration should be given to the particular position the patient occupies in the disease trajectory, ie, the immediate post-detoxification period, the previously treated patient who has slipped, the patient in the subacute phase, etc.

Some of the more important referral options open to the physician include Alcoholics Anonymous (AA); a psychotherapist (psychiatrist, psychologist, social worker); community mental health centers; residential facilities; and social services, ie, Vocational Rehabilitation, Family Services, etc. Referral to any resource should be made as carefully as is a referral to a colleague in another medical specialty.

In making referral for treatment, a major consideration is whether or not the patient can benefit from AA alone, psychotherapy alone, or combined AA and psychotherapy.

Alcoholics Anonymous

Since its inception in 1935, Alcoholics Anonymous has developed as a primary force in the field of alcoholism by articulating the disease concept and by offering a therapeutic milieu for arresting the disease. Most of the information that reaches the lay public and much of the information about alcohol abuse/dependence that reaches practicing physicians is influenced by the perspective of Alcoholics Anonymous. Alcoholics Anonymous influences treatment both as a philosophy and as a method; this organization is fundamental to most public and many private rehabilitation programs for alcohol abuse/dependence.

From the communications media, one can easily derive the concept that Alcoholics Anonymous is the most effective treatment approach for alcoholism. It is necessary to appreciate that AA is different in different areas, differs within a community, and frequently meets the parochial needs of a particular community. The claim that AA is the most effective treatment strategy has never been seriously challenged, nor can it be challenged with an evaluation methodology because of the very nature of its existence (anonymous) and process (unstructured). Although there is no question that AA, as a philosophy of recovery and as a treatment strategy, has been invaluable to many alcoholic patients, one must be cautious in accepting the empirical and universal use of AA as a treatment modality, thereby mandating referral to AA as an absolutely necessary step. It has been suggested that AA may be inappropriate for certain persons who, in the earlier stages of alcohol abuse/dependence, will not necessarily embrace their "powerlessness" over alcohol as an absolute prerequisite to recovery; that is, in some cases, mandating AA involvement may compromise early intervention.

Another issue that has been raised in regard to universal acceptance of Alcoholics Anonymous as a philosophy and as a treatment is the fact that innovation in the field may be obviated. Research efforts and findings in the area of alcohol abuse/dependence are increasing rapidly; many questions are being raised concerning the nature and nurture of the diseases of alcoholism. Frequently, these questions and findings fall on deaf ears. In many areas, Alcoholics Anonymous wants to identify itself, (in some cases only tangentially) with the health care delivery system. A problem exists when a clinical field which purports to use scientific principles and theories in the service of treating the alcohol-abusing/-dependent patient creates a climate in which research findings may be ignored and disregarded.

It should be noted that although AA should not be recommended as a universal approach to *all* patients, there is no treatment approach, given the current state of the art, that can serve as a universal approach.

The fellowship and empathetic milieu of AA can be of invaluable assistance to many patients in the chronic phase. There are several useful guidelines for referral of patients to AA.

First recognize certain characteristics of the patient that may predispose him or her to the benefits of AA fellowship. Those who may benefit are: (a) persons who are comfortable with the identity of the "alcoholic" label as a requisite for improvement and recovery; (b) persons who find meaningfulness by perceiving the similarity of an event to other events (the experience of other AA members) or the similarity of an event to a norm or idea (the AA philosophy); (c) persons who are incapable of, unwilling to or dysfunctionally uncomfortable with the exploration of underlying conflicts and interpersonal dynamics as a major feature of their alcohol abuse/dependence; (d) persons who cannot visualize themselves socializing and having fun outside of a drinking context; (e) persons plagued with severely dependent behaviors (frequently, inordinate dependency needs can be transferred to and more appropriately met by the fellowship of AA); (f) persons who are more likely to accept the spiritual aspects of AA; and (g) persons who have positively responded to AA in the past.

It should be noted that there are really no inclusion or exclusion criteria for predicting treatment outcome in AA. The above characteristics have been useful to me in making an AA referral and, more specifically, in deciding on the particular group within AA to which the patient should be referred.

Second, when making patient referrals, choose a specific individual whom you know from your own experience will offer opportunities for patient identification in sex, age, marital status, ethnic background, socioeconomic and occupational position, personality, and alcoholic history. Such an individual would, in all likelihood, lead the patient to the appropriate AA group. The physician out of contact with AA is unable to make this rational choice for a patient.

Third, discuss in depth the patient's AA experience, both current and past, in order to resolve those difficulties that the patient may raise to resist this therapeutic program. A nonreligious patient may have difficulty with the spiritual aspects of the AA program.

Fourth, the physician can not only acquire necessary clinical training by attending AA meetings, but can influence the local AA membership in various medical matters. The physician may personally make the use of antipsychotic, antidepressant, and disulfiram therapy credible by developing a dialogue with AA group members.

In many cases, forming a liaison with and cooperating with AA can provide assistance to the physician in the initial and long-term management of the patient.[7,8]

Referral to Psychotherapy

Four considerations provide guidelines for referral of the patient for psychotherapy. First, if the physician feels a lack of interest in the psychotherapeutic relationship or unqualified to assume the responsibility, the patient should be referred elsewhere for therapy. Second, recognize certain characteristics of the patient which might predispose him/her to the benefits of psychotherapy. Those who may benefit are persons who are presently ambivalent with or uncomfortable with the identity of the "alcoholic" label as a requisite for improvement and recovery, and persons who find meaningfulness in the cause and effect between an event and other events, norms, and ideals. Third, be certain that the attitude of the psychotherapist (especially a psychiatrist) is nonjudgmental and consonant with the needs of the patient. Be aware of those therapists who, because of hostility toward the "alcoholic" label, will insist upon unrealistic treatment goals. Fourth, the same considerations, in theory, obtain for both individual and group psychotherapy.

Residential Aftercare

Patients who are homeless, whose home situations are volatile and disruptive, or who suffer from significant social instability often require the type of organized therapeutic environment offered by residential aftercare (quarterway or halfway houses). This is frequently preferable to a long-term hospital inpatient stay, since most residential programs encourage early resocialization.

Community Mental Health Centers

Most comprehensive community mental health centers offer alcoholism treatment services that include family therapy and individual and group therapy on both scheduled and nonscheduled bases. These services are designed for patients who have had previous treatment experiences and sufficient family and social stability not to require more protective systems.

Vocational Rehabilitation

Job instability and unemployment are very real and pressing problems to alcoholics. Vocational rehabilitation programs, especially those with specialized services for alcoholics, can offer evaluation of individual needs, personal adjustment, prevocational and vocational training, coordination and integration of rehabilitation services, job placement, case management, and follow-up. Frequently, it is a matter of vocational habilitation rather than rehabilitation.

The issue is a complicated one. First, there is the specific problem of the inner-city alcoholic who lacks job skills and job opportunities. Second, career development, in those less deprived, represents one of the major areas in which a substantive change in self-esteem can be effected. The significance of a basic change in self-image is crucial to the development of long-term sobriety. Physicians should be familiar with the referral guidelines of vocational rehabilitation centers in their areas and should work closely with the counselors involved.

PROGNOSIS

In treating any disease, physicians are trained and sensitized to query themselves continuously on the efficacy of their treatment. "Is my treatment approach helpful?" "Is what I'm doing detrimental to the patient or better than nothing at all?" In thus assessing the efficacy of treatment by the physician and by other resources, it is important to remember that abstinence from alcohol is a means to an end. Recidivism or relapse ("falling off the wagon") does not necessarily imply treatment failure. Specific signs of improvement should be appreciated. Does the patient have a realistic understanding of alcohol dependency in regard to her or his personal situation? Is the patient actively participating in a treatment program? Is there improvement in family and social relationships? Is there improvement in job performance? Is the patient exhibiting longer periods of effective sobriety and (in case of a relapse) are the drinking episodes of shorter duration and less destructive?

Alcoholism, in its many guises and with its many complications, is not a homogeneous disease but rather a disease spectrum. The medical practitioner can assume critical diagnostic and therapeutic roles in the initial and long-term phases of treatment after emergency care and medical management have been afforded the patient. Working with other disciplines in the formulation and implementation of a treatment plan is an essential component of an overall rehabilitation effort and will contribute significantly to the control and recovery of the patient.

REFERENCES

1. Knott DH, Fink RD, Morgan JC: After Detoxification—The physician's role in the initial treatment phase of alcoholism, in Gitlow SE, Peyser Hd (eds): *Alcoholism: A Practical Treatment Guide*. Orlando, Fla, Grune & Stratton, 1980, pp 89–102.
2. Knauert AP: Perspective from a private practice: The differential diagnosis of alcoholism. *Fam Community Health—Alcoholism Health* 2(2) 1:11, 1977.
3. Blane HI: Psychotherapeutic approach, in Kissin B, Begleiter H (eds): *The Biology of Alcoholism: V. Treatment and Rehabilitation of the Chronic Alcoholic*. New York, Plenum, 1977, pp 105–108.
4. Imhof J, Hirsch R, Terenzi RD: Countertransferential and attitudinal considerations in the treatment of drug abuse and addiction. *J Substance Abuse Treatment* 1:21–30, 1984.
5. Knott DH, Thomson MJ, Beard JD: The forgotten addict. *Am Fam Physician* 3: 92–95, 1971.
6. Gitlow SE: Antabuse in Gitlow SE, Peyser HS (eds): *Alcoholism: A Practical Treatment Guide*. Orlando, Fla, Grune & Stratton, 1980, pp 273–278.
7. BW: The fellowship of Alcoholics Anonymous, in Catanzaro RJ (ed): *Alcoholism: The Total Treatment Approach*. Springfield, Illinois, Charles C Thomas, 1968, pp 116–127.
8. Rosen A: Psychotherapy and Alcoholics Anonymous. *Bull Menninger Clin* 45:229–246, 1981.

Chapter 7
ALCOHOL PROBLEMS AND THE FAMILY

The development of the alcoholism treatment enterprise within the past several years to include alcohol-abusing/-dependent patients who are not necessarily homeless, jobless, divorced from spouse, and separated from other family members has elucidated the threat to the family structure. In 1980, a survey conducted by the Gallup Organization revealed that 60% of respondents identified alcohol abuse/dependence as one of the most harmful influences on family viability. Furthermore, 25% of the respondents felt that alcohol abuse/dependence had adversely affected their family.[1]

Although there is general agreement that alcohol abuse/dependence adversely affects family interactions and growth, there is still considerable confusion concerning the realistic assessment, treatment, and expectations of the family affected by alcohol. Until recently, therapy in this regard has originated from clinical empiricism rather than from research data.

Most physicians are familiar with and, in principle, accept family systems theories, which hold that the family is an extraordinary, complex social unit and is the foundation of all societies. The three primary tasks of the family are to provide for the physical survival of family members, the stabilization and growth of parental personalities, and the production of autonomous children and, thereafter (it is hoped) of autonomous adults The family system is further affected by other systems (biochemical, genetic, etc) in its development and maintenance.

ASSESSMENT

The family is considered to be an organizationally structured system that is a dynamic continuum.[2,3]

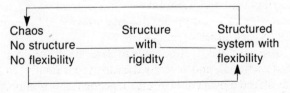

Chaos	Structure	Structured
No structure	with	system with
No flexibility	rigidity	flexibility

There are five essential variables, the assessment of which affects the classification of the family within this continuum as: (a) optimal, (b) competent, (c) mid-range dysfunctional, and (d) severely dysfunctional. These family variables include: structure, mythology, autonomy, capacity for goal-directed negotiation, and affect.

Structure

Assessment in the area of family structure should determine the power distribution in the family. Evaluation involves the nature (strength v weakness) of parent–parent and parent–child coalitions and whether or not such coalitions compromise the power distribution.

Mythology

Family mythology involves the self-concept of each individual family member and the consensual self-concept of the family as a unit when compared with the perceptions of an outside observer, ie, the practicing physician. Frequently, the dysfunctional family may perceive itself as healthy.

Autonomy

Family autonomy involves the extent to which each family member communicates thoughts and feelings to each other and to persons outside the family; the extent to which each family member accepts personal responsibilities for his/her thoughts, feelings, and behaviors; the degree of family permeability, ie, the extent to which family members openly acknowledge each other's thoughts, feelings, and behaviors; and the degree of invasiveness, ie, the extent to which family members speak for each other and "mind read."

Capacity for Goal-Directed Negotiation

Goal-directed negotiation is the ability of family members to listen to the thoughts and feelings of other members and to enter effective intrafamily negotiations toward realistic and consensually agreed-upon goals.

Affect

Affect describes the baseline mood and tone of the family (eg, warm–cold, happy–depressed, etc) and is predominantly influenced by family empathy, ie, sensitivity to each other's feelings.

Utilizing these variables, it is possible to describe the optimal, competent, midrange dysfunctional, and severely dysfunctional family. In those family constellations affected by alcohol abuse/dependence, it is important to ascertain not only the current status of the family, but also the premorbid status. Has there been a deterioration of the dynamic continuum coincident with the onset and progression of alcohol problems? What, historically, has been the highest level of functioning of the family? Answers to such questions assist the physician in formulating realistic expectations in terms of improving family functioning through intervention and treatment.

Optimal Family

In the optimal family, there is clearly defined parental leadership that changes according to the situation. The parents share power without authoritarianism, and parent–child coalitions are designed to encourage the child and adolescent to assume more authority and responsibility under the leadership of parental power.

There is a congruent mythology in the optimal family. That the family is healthy can be easily validated by outside observers.

Among members of the optimal family, there is a high level of closeness without sacrifice of individuality. Thoughts and feelings are expressed with different styles and are mutually respected. Although the parents are generally busy and successful in their own right, there is adequate energy and affect remaining to devote to family members.

In the optimal family, problems are solved effectively and quickly through negotiations involving all family members. The affect is warm, affectionate, and happy, and is evident in both intra-family and extra-family relationships.

It is impossible to identify an optimal family system that is affected by alcohol abuse/dependence. Although this level of family functioning is an ideal goal, it is exceedingly difficult to achieve in any family and particularly in one that is affected by alcohol problems.

The Competent Family

Although there is a high degree of parental competence and obvious parental leadership in the competent family, such leadership does not easily shift according to situations, and the exercise of power vacillates between being authoritative and authoritarian. Parent–child coalitions are occasionally developed to solve problems that exist because of a lack of sharing of power between parents.

The mythology of the competent family is frequently incongruent. The parents are sure that the family is healthy, but their view is not necessarily shared by the children, the adolescents, and outside observers.

Although communications between members of the competent family are usually clear, and although thoughts and feelings are expressed and accepted with respect, the development of individual styles in this regard is not encouraged. Style is usually patterned after the dominant figure in the family.

The parents are usually successful, but often the husband (father) is remote and has little residual energy and affect to devote to the family, leaving the wife (mother) as the person primarily responsible for "raising the children."

Negotiations for problem and conflict resolution in the competent family are often plagued by procrastination and contaminated by the parent–child coalition in lieu of a sharing of power by the parents. The exercise of authority by children and adolescents is often a matter of expediency rather than of design.

The baseline mood of the competent family is one of politeness, but because family empathy is limited, the mood often is troubled. One may occasionally find a family affected by alcohol problems (early stage) to be competent. However, deterioration is usually rapid.

Mid-Range Dysfunctional Family

In terms of power distribution, there are two types of mid-range dysfunctional family. The first is the stable, dominant type in which there is submission of one parent to the more powerful figure (usually the other parent, but sometimes an adolescent). Overt conflict is infrequent. The second is the unstable type in which there is constant conflict and struggle for power between parents. In both types, power often shifts to parent–child coalitions, with marked polarization within the family.

The mythology of the mid-range dysfunctional family is incongruent. The attitude expressed by family members is, "I'm okay, but other family members are not." Scapegoating is common. There is little closeness and intimacy; lack of respect for feelings and thoughts of others both within and outside the family compromises individuality. Feelings are masked, and there is a high degree of invasiveness, ie, family members "mind read" and speak for each other.

In the mid-range dysfunctional family, there is almost no negotiation; problem-solving is accomplished through the use of raw power, which can be assumed by any family member, ie, parent, adolescent, or child.

Baseline mood is angry, depressed, and sullen, with almost total lack of sensitivity to each other's feelings.

It is very common to find that families affected by alcohol abuse/dependence fall into the mid-range dysfunctional classification. Unless family ties dissolve or are restructured among the patient and other family members, the severely dysfunctional level is reached.

Severely Dysfunctional Family

There is absolutely no parental leadership in the severely dysfunctional family. Parent–parent coalitions are weak and usually are insignificant as compared with extremely powerful parent–child coalitions.

Paradoxically, there is a congruent mythology in the severely dysfunctional family in that the individual and collective impression is that the family is unhealthy, and pathology is rampant, a condition easily validated by outside observers.

There is no communication of or respect for thoughts and feelings. No family member accepts responsibility for thoughts, feelings, and behaviors. Autonomy is disorganized; fusion (taking sides) is common.

There is almost no capacity for goal-directed negotiation. Problem-solving is grossly inefficient and, when accomplished, is done through the power of parent–child coalitions.

The baseline mood of a severely dysfunctional family is angry, cynical, and hopeless.

In essence, the severely dysfunctional family system is characterized by never-ending chaos.

If families affected by untreated alcohol abuse/dependence remain geographically intact, they are at high risk of becoming severely dysfunctional. Early recognition of and intervention for the family troubled with alcohol problems may prevent the progression to the severely dysfunctional stage; once this stage is reached, treatment for the family is often futile.

Using the assessment paradigm outlined above, it is possible to define themes in families affected by alcohol problems. Although there are variations between families, there is now sufficient knowledge to allow for generalizations. The following discussion is based on families in which the husband is affected by alcohol, since little research has been done in regard to the alcoholic wife within a family system. In addition, the nonalcoholic husband more often denies and camouflages his wife's drinking than does the wife the husband's drinking. The lack of research data probably results from the perception that for every ten alcoholic husbands, nine of the wives will remain in the marriage; obversely, for every ten alcoholic wives, only one of the husbands will remain in the marriage. However, some of the following generalizations are valid, regardless of which spouse is alcohol-dependent.[4-6]

The Family Affected by Alcohol Problems

The axiom that a family is an autocracy ruled by its sickest member is pertinent to the issue of power distribution. In parental power, three processes may be operational within the structure of the family affected by alcohol problems.

First, the nonalcoholic spouse has a need for the alcohol-dependent partner to continue drinking in order to assume a presumed dominant position and to cope with her own feelings of inadequacy. The wife will alternate between playing the roles of persecutor and rescuer when relating to the alcohol-dependent spouse (the victim). At the core of this role reversal is the motivation to remain in control. Paradoxically, it frequently is the "sick" family member who is in constant control.

Second, the parent–parent relationship, which is compromised by alcohol, actually is a relationship plagued with many problems associated with power distribution and power sharing; such problems, although blamed on alcohol, would exist without alcohol. Often, even when sobriety is achieved within the family, these problems are still evident and often escalate in severity.

Third, both parents consciously compete for power, the alcohol abuser by the continued but often intermittent use of alcohol and the spouse by withdrawn and dependent behaviors. Neither parent emerges as the dominant figure, giving rise to powerful parent–child coalitions that are the most significant factor in problem-solving efforts. The lack of parental leadership often results in the adoption of illness behaviors by the child or adolescent so that the "sickest" member of the family can still be the ruler of the autocracy.

For most successful treatment, attention must be paid to the interactional processes and not only to the alcohol-abusing member.

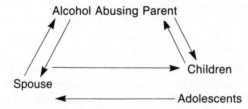

Members of the family affected by alcohol may attempt to perceive and portray a mythology of the family constellation as healthy in order to deny the problem and to avoid dealing with each individual's responsibility for and resistance to change. The outside observer can quickly recognize the absence of family health. The family mythology is incongruent.

Any autonomy—closeness and intimacy—that does exist results from attempts to understand and cope with the illness behaviors of the alcohol-abusing parent. Emotional polarization is common and depends on whether or not the family is "dry" (abstinent) or "wet" (drinking) and which phase—ie, persecution or rescuing is the predominant process of interaction between family members with the "victim." Thoughts and feelings are poorly communicated and often repressed. There is often an unwarranted assumption of responsibility for "causing and curing" the alcohol problem on the part of other family members, which leads to guilt, anger, and frustration.

Frequently, the only goal that is established in family negotiations is abstinence from alcohol for the affected parent. If abstinence is achieved, it is then perceived with ambivalence by all family members because of the vacillating and ineffective power distribution within the family and the continued quest for control. This singular goal obviates recognition of other nonalcoholrelated goals, and thus intra-family negotiations are almost nonexistent. The baseline mood of the family affected by alcohol is angry, depressed, and influenced by a pseudo-empathy. The discharge of family affect is unpredictable and inappropriate. Affective energy focuses solely on the drinking behaviors; often more energy is expended on the transformation of affect into its opposite: the facade of happiness to cover depression, caring to cover anger, warmth to cover cold. This is psychologically expensive to all members of the family.

TREATMENT

Just as the disease concept of alcoholism is not necessarily a unitary phenomenon, neither is the relationship between alcohol abuse/dependence and family problems a single, unitary process. The following discussion is intended to offer concepts and suggestions concerning treatment of the family affected by alcohol problems, keeping in mind that therapy should be designed with both eclecticism and individualism.[7,8,9]

Homeostasis

The family system is a homeostatic mechanism designed to resist change over long periods of time. Therapeutic attempts that intend to change individual and collective behaviors threaten family homeostasis and often lead to an increase in illness behaviors on the part of all family members in order to maintain the status quo. In many cases, drinking (and other illness behaviors) may be perceived by family members as stabilizing rather than a disruptive influence on homeostasis. As pathological as the alcohol abuse may appear to the therapist, such abuse may well be the "glue" holding the family together. The physician should anticipate and be prepared to deal with the possibility of further family disintegration even though abstinence from alcohol is achieved. Behaviors that appear maladaptive to the physician are often adaptive to the family functioning; one must search for the secondary gains such behaviors provide and encourage more healthy behaviors to stabilize the homeostasis. From a physiological point of view, homeostatic mechanisms are often "set" at different levels. In many cases, it is essential to "reset" the homeostatic level (expectations) of the family, ie, to move from mid-range dysfunctional level to competent level.

Improving Family Function

All family members are instrumental in improving the treatment of the identified alcohol-dependent patient. The family should be viewed as the "patient." Intervention must focus on all intra-family interactions, not only the identified patient. The treatment goal, therefore, is improvement of family functioning and growth as a whole rather than mere reduction of the drinking in the identified patient. Defining existing problems in family structure, mythology, capacity for negotiations, autonomy, and affect is valuable in establishing treatment strategies and realistic goals for improvement.

Family Therapy

In some instances, the identified parent will refuse treatment. Therapy should still be afforded to other family members, since their continued support of and participation in the drinking and other illness behaviors only perpetuates the dysfunction. Modifying family relationships frequently results in significant improvement in family functioning, even though the identified patient has not participated in the formal treatment process, which should focus on interaction, communication, role performances, and problem definition of the family rather than the individual.

Individual and Collective Therapy

While treatment is directed toward the family as a system, techniques should be tailored to treat the identified patient, the spouse, the marriage, the children, and the adolescents both on an individual and collective basis, depending on the problems and circumstances.

Involvement of Extended Family

Important to the homeostasis of the nuclear family are interactional patterns established with members of the extended family. Frequently, relatives, either wittingly or unwittingly, become involved in the family conflicts and often "take sides." There may be a pathological dependency on parents and relatives, not only by the alcohol-dependent member, but also by the spouse. This pathological dependency may have preceded the onset of alcohol problems but certainly can be consequential to these problems. Changing these dependencies is difficult and necessitates expansion of treatment efforts to include important members of the extended family within the system.

Kinship Systems

In conceptualizing the field of family therapy, evaluation and treatment efforts should be expanded beyond the scope of just the family (nuclear and extended) system to include the psychosocial kinship system as well.[9] This implies working with friends, neighbors, work associates, church associates, and recreational associates when those relationships seem significant. This is certainly applicable to working with families affected by alcohol problems, since, in many cases, powerful coalitions are formed between family members and others outside the family. In fact, in many cases, the basic social system is founded in the extended psychosocial kinship system rather than within the nuclear and extended families.

Referral

Referral of family members to Al-Anon (self-help group for spouses of the alcohol-dependent family member), Alateen (self-help group for children and adolescents with an alcoholic parent(s), and the relatively new Ala-Fam (self-help group for nuclear and extended family members within a system compromised by alcohol abuse/dependence) can be extremely helpful to the physician who is involved with families affected by alcohol. If such groups are inactive in a particular community, the physician should act as a catalyst for the formation of such efforts not only in the community, but also in the physician's own practice.

Other Sources

Family therapy is no longer an empirical treatment modality. It requires training and the acquisition of new skills. The busy physician should not hesitate to enlist the assistance of persons from other disciplines (eg, social workers, psychologists, the clergy) in dealing with the family troubled by alcohol.

Because the American family is undergoing some dramatic changes in integrity and style, it is obvious that a single family therapy approach is not feasible.

The medical model and family therapy model for the treatment of alcohol abuse/dependence are not mutually exclusive phenomena as some would suggest; integration rather than separation of these two models is the only meaningful approach to treating families affected by alcohol problems.

No longer can treatment be confined to just the identified patient who has an intact family. Therapeutic attention directed toward the patient, spouse, offspring, biological relatives, and significant others in the psychosocial kinship system should not only enhance the chances of recovery for both the patient and the system, but may prevent the future intergenerational transmission of alcohol abuse/dependence.

REFERENCES

1. *Alcohol and the Family.* National Clearinghouse for Alcohol Information, NIAAA Publication No. (RPO) 311. Rockville, Maryland, 1980.
2. Lewis J: Family assessment in evaluating the adolescent. *Audio Digest* 7(18), 1978.

ALCOHOL PROBLEMS AND THE FAMILY

3. Steinglass P: Experimenting with family treatment approaches to alcoholism 1950–1975: A review. *Fam Process* 15(1):97–123, 1975.
4. Bondreau RJ: Alcohol abuse and the family system. *Canada's Mental Health* June, 17–18, 1982.
5. Kaufman E, Pattison EM: The family and alcoholism, in Pattison EM, Kaufman E (eds): *Encyclopedic Handbook of Alcoholism.* New York, Gardner, 1982, pp 663–672.
6. Knight JA: The family in the crisis of alcoholism, in Gitlow SE, Peyser HS (eds): *Alcoholism: A Practical Treatment Guide.* Orlando, Fla, Grune & Stratton, 1980, pp 205–228.
7. Janzen C: Family treatment for alcoholism: A review. *Soc Work* 27 (March):135–141, 1982.
8. Kaufman E, Pattison EM: Family and network therapy in alcoholism, in Pattison EM, Kaufman E (eds): *Encyclopedic Handbook of Alcoholism.* New York, Gardner, pp 1022–1032, 1982.
9. Pattison EM, DeFrancisco D, Wood P, et al: A psychosocial kinship model for family therapy. *Am J Psychiatry* 132:1246–1251, 1975.

Chapter 8
ALCOHOL USE AND SPECIAL POPULATIONS

Fortunately, in the last decade there has been increased awareness that alcohol use, alcohol abuse, and alcohol dependence exhibit some pathogenetic differences between special populations. Previously, the knowledge base on which attitudes, treatment concepts, and prognostic expectations concerning alcoholism were based derived from studies on adult, Caucasian males, aged >40 years, who were treated in the state hospital systems. The difficulty in utilizing this knowledge base when dealing with special populations such as women, adolescents, the elderly, minorities, etc, is now apparent. Appreciation of the diagnostic and treatment nuances indigenous to special populations is essential to skillful and well-informed patient care.

The following is a brief and certainly not exhaustive discussion of alcohol problems in special populations, with emphasis on the fetus, adolescents, women, the elderly, and physicians.

Selection of these populations is based on my experience and is certainly not inclusive of all the special populations. To simplify the discussion, consideration will be given to the following areas for each population: (a) alcohol history; (b) physiological description; (c) psychological description; (d) social description; (e) treatment considerations; and (f) prevention implications. Although generalizations are made, it is noted that there can be wide variations in the above areas within each population.

THE FETUS

Historical recognition that alcohol may have teratogenetic effects is well exemplified by an ancient Carthaginian mandate: "The bridal couple was forbidden to drink wine on their wedding night in order that defective children might not be conceived." However, this issue has received appropriate attention in this country only in the past 10 to 15 years, with a growing number of clinical reports dealing with the fetal alcohol syndrome (FAS). As a result of stimulated research interest, data now suggest that maternal alcohol use can cause not only FAS, but also alcohol-related birth defects (ARBD), which are more subtle but which nevertheless can produce considerable dysfunction and impairment.[1]

Alcohol History

Original observations of fetal abnormalities attributed to maternal alcohol use were made in women who appeared to be clearly alcohol-dependent and who drank heavily during pregnancy.[2,3] Although a zealous search for "safe drinking patterns" in pregnant women continues, some investigators warn that "a continuum of increased risk for adverse effects is related to increasing levels of alcohol consumption, ranging from one to two drinks per day on the average up to maternal alcoholism."[4] In addition, there are recent claims that growth deficiency, morphologic abnormalities, and central nervous system (CNS) dysfunction have been associated with self-reported maternal doses of alcohol between one and four drinks per day. In addition to the teratogenicity of alcohol, there have been a number of consequences attributed to the in utero toxicity of alcohol, ie, an increased incidence of stillbirths and spontaneous abortions, the latter occurring in the second trimester three times more frequently in women who consume three or more drinks per day than in those who consume less than one drink daily. In addition, it is speculated that the direct CNS toxicity of alcohol in the fetus can result in impairment in newborn conditioning and in permanent cognitive and behavioral abnormalities.[5,6]

Physiological Description

Early detection of cases of FAS is not difficult. However, there appears to be a continuum of abnormalities, the severity of which is, in part, dose-dependent. The characteristics of the FAS and, in milder cases, ARBD, are outlined in Tables 8.1 and 8.2.

Psychological Description

It is becoming increasingly clear that psychological and behavioral abnormalities can exist with only minimal malformation or even in the absence of physical malformations. Mental retardation is one of the most common and serious problems associated with FAS and is usually accompanied by physical abnormalities. However, there appears to be a close association between maternal alcohol use and the increased incidence of hyperactivity in childhood and adolescence, suggesting a link between attention deficit disorders and drinking during pregnancy. Indeed, the "behavioral teratology" of alcohol may prove to be a more serious problem than the full-blown clinical picture

Table 8 1 Principal Features of the Fetal Alcohol Syndrome.

Feature	Manifestation
Central Nervous System Dysfunction	
Intellectual	Mild to moderate mental retardation*
Neurological	Microcephaly*
	Poor coordination, hypotonia†
Behavioral	Irritability in infancy*
	Hyperactivity in childhood†
Growth Deficiency	
Prenatal	>2 SD for length and weight*
Postnatal	>2 SD for length and weight*
	Disproportionately diminished adipose tissue†
Facial Characteristics	
Eyes	Short palpebral fissures*
Nose	Short, upturned†
	Hypoplastic philtrum*
Maxilla	Hypoplastic†
Mouth	Thinned upper vermilion*
	Retrognathia in infancy*
	Micrognathia or relative prognathia in adolescence†

*Denotes feature seen in >80% of patients.
†Denotes feature seen in >50% of patients.

of FAS.[7,8] It has been postulated that certain cases of schizophrenia may be a psychiatric consequence of FAS or ARBD. Certainly, further data are needed to delineate more clearly the long-term cognitive–behavioral–affective consequences of maternal alcohol use on the offspring. At this juncture, it is reasonable to assume that the CNS teratogenicity and toxicity of alcohol does indeed result in psychiatric consequences.

Social Description

Although the incidence of FAS and ARBD is reportedly higher in the lower socioeconomic population (American Indians and children of older mothers), prospective epidemiological studies involving most ethnic, racial, and socioeconomic groups reveal that FAS and ARBD can indeed affect all groups, the apparent common denominator being maternal alcohol use, with the probability of a dose-dependent phenomenon.

Treatment Considerations

Because most of the adverse effects of alcohol on the fetus are essentially irreversible, treatment is, at best, palliative for the affected individuals. Treatment of the alcohol-dependent mother during pregnancy may reduce the risk of toxicity and, to a lesser extent, the teratogenicity of alcohol; however, the most serious CNS complications appear to occur during the first trimester, often before the woman is aware of the pregnancy.

Table 8.2. Associated Features of the Fetal Alcohol Syndrome.

Area	Frequent	Occasional
Eyes	Ptosis, strabismus epicanthal folds	Myopia, clinical micropthalmia, blepharophimosis
Ears	Posterior rotation	Poorly formed concha
Mouth	Prominent lateral	Cleft lip or cleft palate, small teeth with faulty enamel
Cardiac	Murmurs, especially in childhood, usually atrial septal defect	Ventricular septal defect, great vessel anomalies, tetralogy of Fallot
Renogenital	Labial hypoplasia	Hypospadias, small rotated kidneys, hydronephrosis
Cutaneous	Hemangiomas	Hirsutism in infancy
Skeletal	Aberrant palmar creases, pectus excavatum	Limited joint movements, especially fingers and elbows; nail hypoplasia, especially fifth nail, polydactly; radioulnar synostosis; pectus carinatum; bifid xiphoid; Kleppel-Feil anomaly; scoliosis
Muscular		Hernias of diaphragm, umbilicus or groin; diastasis recti

Prevention Considerations

Warnings against the use of alcohol in pregnant women that have been promulgated by the AMA, NIAAA, and the Surgeon General have provoked both controversy and confusion. Certainly, additional studies which focus on complicating factors in addition to maternal alcohol use, such as concomitant nicotine use, other drug use, drinking patterns (constant v binge drinking), use of caffeine, etc, are needed before one can state with absolute certainty that maternal alcohol use is the sole cause of FAS and ARBD. Until the issue is clearly resolved, all physicians should become knowledgeable about the major recommendations (quoted below) of the AMA in this regard.[7]

1. The evidence is clear that a woman who drinks heavily during pregnancy places her unborn child at substantial risk for fetal damage and physical and mental deficiencies in infancy. Physicians should be alert to signs of possible alcohol abuse and alcoholism in their female patients of childbearing age, not only those who are pregnant, and institute appropriate diagnostic and therapeutic measures as early as possible. Prompt intervention may prevent adverse fetal consequences from occurring in this high-risk group.

2. The fetal risks involved in moderate or minimal alcohol consumption have not been established through research to date, nor has a safe level of maternal alcohol use. One of the objectives of future research should be to determine whether there is a level of maternal alcohol consumption below which embryotoxic and teratogenic effects attributable to alcohol are virtually non-existent.

3. Until such a determination is made, physicians should inform their patients as to what the research to date does and does not show, and should encourage them to decide about drinking in light of the evidence and their own situations. Physicians should be explicit in reinforcing the concept that, with several aspects of the issue still in doubt, *the safest course is abstinence.*

4. Long-term longitudinal studies should be undertaken to give a clearer perception of the nature and duration of alcohol-related birth defects. Cooperative projects should be designed with uniform means of assessing the quantity and extent of alcohol intake.

5. To enhance public education efforts, schools, hospitals and community organizations should become involved in programs conducted by governmental agencies and professional associations.

6. Physicians themselves should take an active part in education campaigns, such as the one being sponsored by NIAAA. In so doing, they should emphasize the often-overlooked consequences of maternal drinking that are less dramatic and pronounced than are features of the fetal alcohol syndrome, consequences that are at least indicated, if not sharply delineated, by some of the research that has been conducted in several parts of the world with diverse populations.

ADOLESCENTS

There is a growing consensus that there are major conceptual differences between alcohol problems in adolescents and those in the adult population. For instance, there are fewer alcohol-related medical problems in the adolescent; the adolescent is more insulated from role performance areas; and alcohol use in adolescents is a behavior more closely integrated into the developmental process — it is viewed as a part of a general developmental adaptation to self, others, and situations rather than as an isolated and necessarily deviant behavior. Diagnostic criteria applicable to alcohol dependence in adults may be only partly relevant to problem drinking in adolescents in regard to implied pathology.

Alcohol History

Considerable controversy continues to surround the incidence and prevalence of drinking problems (alcohol use v misuse) in adolescents. Traditional techniques for gathering such data in adults such as self-questionnaires, medical consequences, number of persons in treatment, and death rates are of limited value in assessing the problem in adolescents. Perhaps the most revealing survey data in this regard derives from the Adolescent Alcohol Involvement Scale developed by Mayer and Filstead, designed to differentiate adolescents into four groups[9]: (a) adolescents who completely abstain or who use alcohol at a minimal level; (b) adolescents who use alcohol but who do not experience or display any associated problem behaviors; (c) adolescents who use alcohol and experience obvious associated problems; and (d) adolescents who use alcohol and experience problems to the degree found in patients who are being treated for alcohol dependence.

Results of surveys using this paradigm indicate the following percentages within each group: 5% in group 1, abstinent or minimal use; 71% in group 2, alcohol use not associated with problems; 19% in group 3, alcohol use associated with significant problems (ie, academic, social, legal, family); and 5% in group 4, alcohol use which creates problems similar to those experienced by patients in treatment.

Many people have surmised that the increasing attention being paid to adolescent alcohol use is tantamount to a sudden and significant escalation in problem drinking. A review of the literature reveals the following[9,10]:

1. Since 1965, there is a trend toward alcohol consumption at an earlier age.
2. There is no evidence that more adolescents are using alcohol now than in previous generations.
3. Since 1975, it appears that more adolescent females are using alcohol, and the male-female ratio in terms of numbers of users is approximating 1.
4. There appears to be a trend toward increased amounts of alcohol consumed by adolescents, partly due to an earlier initial drinking age.
5. Attitudes toward alcohol use appear to be formed at an early age, ie, 8 to 10 years, and the average age of initial ingestion of alcohol appears to be 11 years.

Psychological Description

The sociopsychological model as explained by Donovan and Jessor[11] is a sensible paradigm that offers better understanding of drinking and problem drinking in adolescents. If one assumes that the construct is a problem-behavioral model, there are three variables which are operational: (a) the personality of the adolescent; (b) the environment as perceived by the adolescent; and (c) the behavior patterns of the adolescent. Utilizing these variables, research designed to delineate critical differences between problem and nonproblem adolescent drinkers revealed the following characteristics of the problem-drinking population.

Personality

In contrast to nonproblem drinkers, problem drinkers (a) place less value on academic achievement; (b) place greater value on independence and personal autonomy; (c) place greater value on independence relative to achievement; (d) have lower expectations of achievement; (e) are more tolerant of deviance; (f) are less religious; and (g) place more importance on the positive than on the negative functions of drinking.

Perceived Environment

In contrast to nonproblem drinkers, problem drinkers (a) perceive less compatibility between their peer group and their parents; (b) are more easily influenced by peers than by parents; and (c) perceive more pressure for drinking and drug use.

Behavioral Patterns

In contrast to nonproblem drinkers, problem drinkers (a) are more involved in deviant behavior; (b) smoke more marijuana; (c) are less involved in religious activities; (d) are less involved in conventional social institutions and activities; and (e) have a lower academic achievement.

The above model is compatible with the conduct disorders of adolescence. However, secondary alcohol abuse/dependence can be manifest in the adolescent, particularly in those with the primary diagnosis of identity disorder, schizoid disorder, affective disorder, borderline syndrome, attention deficit disorder, or anxiety disorder.

It is important to remember that primary alcohol dependence can be manifest during adolescence when there is a positive family history of primary alcohol dependence and especially when alcohol use begins at an earlier age.

When the causative conditions involved with adolescent alcohol use and abuse are explored, the following are considered important factors[12]:

1. Peer group pressure and/or family breakdown
2. Need for symbolic expression of the rites of passage into adulthood
3. Solving of moral dilemmas
4. Search for identity (including a sexual identification)
5. Rejection of social norms and values
6. Coping with aggressive impulses; boredom or apathy
7. Overcoming personal inhibition, anxiety, and depression generated in a competitive society
8. Increased sociability – entertainment
9. An alternative to drugs
10. A search for meaning and purpose in life

Social Description

In regard to social settings and influences that affect adolescent drinking, the home is the most frequent location for drinking. The drinking cohort is composed of friends and peers more than of parents or relatives; however, when drinking is introduced to the adolescent (or child) by parents, there may be fewer problems than if drinking is introduced by peers.

One frequently hears: "My son (daughter) is drinking too much because he (she) fell in with the wrong crowd." It is important to realize that attitudes and early drinking behaviors are usually shaped by the parents and relatives rather than by peers; subsequently, the adolescent frequently seeks that peer group whose attitudes, behaviors, and values are compatible with those already formed through parental influence. Adolescents who tend to seek peer groups that are involved in problem drinking generally come from homes in which there is less parental disapproval of drinking and in which the parents are less involved with and less affectionate toward the adolescent.

In regard to other sociocultural parameters, problem drinking is more highly correlated with an urban setting and a higher socioeconomic status (SES) of the family.

Again, I emphasize that family and social factors at an early preadolescent age appear to be highly significant in the development or nondevelopment of problem drinking, such significance having important treatment and prevention implications.

Treatment Considerations

Considering that confusion and controversy still plague the diagnosis and treatment of adult alcohol abuse/dependence, it is little wonder that the appropriate management of the adolescent problem drinker needs further exploration.

The following are salient albeit somewhat global factors which relate to treatment strategies.

Diagnostically, one must remember that alcohol use and problem drinking in the adolescent is part of a general developmental adaptation to self, others, and situations rather than an isolated and necessarily distinct pathological entity. Thus, developmental issues must be addressed in formulating an individualized treatment approach. Although the drinking may create social problems and appear to be self-destructive, it is imperative to identify the secondary gains of such drinking behaviors as these relate to developmental issues.

Because early attitudes and drinking behaviors are significantly influenced by parents (or caretaking relatives), involvement of these persons in the assessment and treatment process is important.

Adolescent and young adult AA groups have been very helpful in shifting social support systems and peer influence. Generally, adolescents do not relate well to AA groups with older adults.

Be certain that the diagnosis identifies any bona fide disorder of adolescence, ie, attention deficit disorder, conduct disorder, anxiety disorder, affective disorder, etc. Recent evidence suggests that conduct disorders, a very common diagnostic label used with adolescents, may, in many cases, actually be an affective (mood) disorder of significant severity. The obvious implication is that the psychiatric disorder should be treated as vigorously as the problem drinking. Secondary alcohol abuse/dependence can affect adolescents as well as adults.

Treatment of problem-drinking adolescents is usually best accomplished in a milieu with other adolescents rather than in an admixture of adults and adolescents.

As with adults, there must be a wide range and variety of services, the core of which should include: (a) inpatient medical and psychiatric care – preferably in an adolescent unit; (b) free-standing residential treatment programs; (c) alternative living arrangements; and (d) peer counseling programs. The portal of entry should be the least restrictive environment that is compatible with the extent of medical–psychiatric–social problems and the extent and nature of the past, current, and anticipated family and social support systems.

Prevention Considerations

If one considers prevention as a primary process, with secondary and tertiary prevention being early intervention and treatment, the first and most important question to address is the thing to be prevented and in whom. It is unrealistic to "prevent" alcohol use in adolescents. A more appropriate target might be prevention of problem drinking in youth.

Previously, it has been falsely assumed that education is synonymous with prevention. Initial efforts involving "scare tactics" about the toxicity of alcohol were a futile process which has been repeated for thousands of years and were doomed to failure. Subsequently, the "information transmission" approach was taken; facts about alcohol use and abuse were presented objectively to children and adolescents. This approach made little impact on the incidence of alcohol use and problem drinking, since it considered alcohol issues as separate from the developmental process mentioned previously.

A more recent advance in the education–prevention area is the "responsible decision-making approach." This embraces the techniques of affective skills development, which includes improvement of self-concept, appreciation of the values and attitudes held by others, decision-making skills, development of responsibility for self and others, encouragement of creative activity, and preparation to cope with a changing world. Issues relating to drinking and drug-taking behavior, sexual behavior, overly aggressive behaviors, etc, are integrated into the above paradigm rather than separated from it.

The responsibility of implementing the responsible decision-making approach must be shared by the family unit, the school system, the church, and community organizations. This implies that persons of all ages and from many environments become involved in learning such techniques and in serving as healthy role models.

In addition to considering the child and adolescent population at large, special efforts should be mounted in dealing with children and adolescents with alcohol and/or drug-dependent parents, since this appears to be the population at highest risk for developing the addictive diseases in adulthood. Perhaps this new decision-making approach should be applied more intensively to this group.

The physician who assumes responsibility for the care of families should take special care with children and adolescents who have alcohol-dependent parents in assessing developmental progress and in educating them concerning the particular risk factors involved.

With the increasing attention now being directed toward adolescent alcohol use, future research should provide a better understanding between this phenomenon and the development of adult alcohol dependence, an understanding which should improve diagnosis and treatment in this field.

WOMEN

Perhaps there is no other group that has been more plagued with the "male disease" concept of alcoholism than alcohol-dependent women.[13] Recent emphasis on the woman alcoholic has led to the assumption that alcohol dependence in women is a relatively new phenomenon and that the incidence of the alcoholisms in women has rapidly escalated during the past few years. Current estimates place the male–female ratio for alcohol dependence at 4 : 1, although this number may approach 2 : 1 or even 1 : 1 in private practice. Although a modest increase in the incidence of female alcohol dependence may be occurring, other factors such as a new awareness of women, increased visibility of women, the ability of women to drink more openly without being stigmatized, and an increased willingness of these women to seek treatment play important roles in this area.

Alcohol History

Realizing that there is no such thing as the "typical woman alcoholic," generalized comparisons nevertheless have been made between the drinking patterns of men and women. Women usually start drinking and begin drinking heavily at a later age, although this trend may be reversed by the emerging class of young working women. Onset of alcohol-related problems also occurs later. Some other salient differences which have impact on identification and treatment include:

1. Women experience fewer "blackouts" but more suicide attempts.
2. Women are more often solitary drinkers and experience fewer drinking binges.
3. Women are less aggressive, exhibit less drunken-driving behavior, and are arrested less frequently for alcohol-related offenses. (This may represent a selective bias on the part of law enforcement officers.)
4. The course of alcohol dependence appears to be more telescoped in women, ie, a more rapid psychological–physiological–social deterioration.
5. The rate of divorce is much higher in alcohol-dependent women.
6. Abuse of psychoactive drugs in combination with alcohol is more common in women.
7. Morbidity and mortality appear to be higher in alcohol-dependent women.

Diverse theories have been advanced which address the etiology of alcohol dependence in women.[14]

One theory suggests that women who are alcohol-dependent are overwhelmed by intense and unresolved dependency needs and conflicts, with a repressed, but unresolved need for maternal care. One explanation for the larger number of men v women alcoholics is that women are better able to be dependent in our society.

The theory of need for power prevails with regard to male alcohol dependence; however, with the changing posture of women in our society to that of a more competitive role, the disinhibiting effects of alcohol in regard to enhancing aggressive behaviors and fantasies of omnipotence may become increasingly important.

A third theory suggests that the alcohol-dependent woman has a strong ambivalence toward her femininity and doubts about her adequacy as a woman. Theoretically, alcohol ameliorates this ambivalence and doubt, and enhances her sense of femininity, making the woman drinker feel more "womanly."

Another theory holds that alcohol is used by women in coping with life crises — particularly those that may be defeminizing. Life crises that have been associated with the onset of heavy drinking in women are: (a) separation and divorce; (b) death of the mate; (c) extramarital affair of the mate; (d) obstetrical and gynecological problems, (spontaneous abortion, infertility, mastectomy, hysterectomy); (e) the "empty nest syndrome," a time when the role of the woman as a wife and mother is undergoing radical change; and (f) death of a parent, particularly the mother, who characteristically has been cold and dominating.

Consonant with the disease concept of the "alcoholisms," multiple etiologies and clinical manifestations are operational.

Physiological Description

There appear to be some physiological mechanisms operational in women that affect alcohol metabolism and may be pertinent to the onset and development of alcohol dependence.[15,16]

Blood Alcohol Concentrations (BACs) and Sex Hormones

Women achieve a higher blood alcohol concentration with a given gram per kilogram dose of alcohol than men. Presumably, this is due to the fact that the total body water in women is 45% to 50% of body weight, whereas that in men is 55% to 65%. Alcohol distributes in the total body water and thus becomes more diluted in men, who have a greater muscle mass (higher water content) and less adipose tissue (lower water content) than women.

Levels of sex hormones in women appear to have more significant impact on alcohol metabolism than do comparable levels in men. High estrogen levels such as seen in women taking oral contraceptives or at certain times during the menstrual cycle decreases the rate of alcohol metabolism. Differing blood alcohol concentrations (BACs) consequent to a standard gram per kilogram dose of ethanol vary during the menstrual cycle and vary between the premenstrual and postmenstrual periods. Although higher estrogen levels decrease the rate of alcohol metabolism, low estrogen levels are associated with achievement of a higher BAC with a standard gram per kilogram dose of alcohol. Thus, during the immediate premenstrual period and during the menopausal and postmenopausal periods when estrogen levels are falling and/or low, drinking will effect a greater degree of intoxication.

Estrogen is known to have monoamine oxidase-inhibiting properties. Thus, with low estrogen levels, there is a relative increase in MAO activity, which could explain in part the depression associated with the premenstrual phase and postmenopausal periods. This change in affect is viewed by many as a psychological cue for alcohol use, at a time when greater degrees of intoxication occur with a given dose of alcohol.

These physiological mechanisms may partially explain the clinical observation that the response to alcohol in women varies more from drinking episode to drinking episode and is less predictable with an established dose of alcohol than that noted in men.

Although the evidence is somewhat equivocal, there has been a consensus that the incidence and extent of medical complications is more serious in women than in men. Specifically, women drinkers suffer a relatively higher incidence of severe liver disease (cirrhosis and alcoholic hepatitis), anemia, and peripheral neuropathy. There appears to be a significantly higher mortality rate among female than male alcohol-dependent persons. The apparent increase in both morbidity and mortality in alcohol-dependent women places great importance on early diagnosis and aggressive intervention for the population.

Psychological Description

There is a general assumption, partially supported by the anecdotal and research literature, that alcohol-dependent women are "psychologically sicker and more deviant" than alcohol-dependent men. The argument for this assumption is that if excessive drinking by women is viewed culturally as a social taboo and an obvious deviation from accepted behavior, only women with significant psychopathology would exhibit such behavior.

Although the genetic predisposition for alcohol dependence does not appear to be as clear for women as for men, the impact of family factors on the developmental phase of women who become alcohol-dependent may be more influential than for men. During childhood women who become alcoholics sense a greater loss associated with deprivation and disruption, such as a loss of parent by desertion, divorce, or death. In addition, the parental background of alcohol-dependent women is often characterized by a cold, dominating, rejecting mother and a rather passive, indulgent (frequently alcoholic) father. Consequently, such women lack preparation to assume the responsibility of an adult.[17]

Genetic factors in addition to early deprivation may also explain the higher incidence of affective disorders (particularly depression) in women. Secondary alcohol dependence superimposed on an underlying affective disorder occurs more frequently in women, which can explain why alcohol-dependent women are more likely to be admitted to hospitals as psychiatric patients.

Clinical observations additionally suggest that alcohol-dependent women have a lower self-concept and more sexual identity problems than do alcoholic men.

As noted previously, alcohol abuse/dependence in women is frequently associated with specific psychological stressors and life crises. Identification of these stressors and crises and psychotherapeutic assistance to help the patient cope without alcohol contitute an essential treatment approach.

Social Description

There is a broader knowledge base in regard to alcohol-dependent women from lower socioeconomic backgrounds, particularly those in state hospitals and prisons, since it is their drinking that attracts more public attention. When one considers demographic variables, however, the association between drinking practices and socioeconomic status is more pronounced for women than for men.

Alcohol-dependent women in a higher socioeconomic status are generally older, experience a later age of onset of alcohol dependence, are more likely to be continuous drinkers rather than binge drinkers, are less likely to lose friends or a job, are less likely to be arrested, and are hidden by their families to a greater degree.

Alcohol-dependent women in the middle and lower socioeconomic status groups are usually younger, experience more childhood and marital disruption, have more unstable employment histories, more familial alcoholism, more medical complications, and are more prone to binge drinking.

It is likely that as the number of women joining the work force continues to increase, current views concerning the natural history of alcohol dependence in women will change. Initial impressions suggest that the drinking patterns and characteristics of alcohol dependency in the cohort of employed women are indeed similar to those found in employed men.

A major impact of the equal rights for women movement and the growing work group of women is to force a critical appraisal of the double standard of what constitutes a "healthy" man and a "healthy" woman. As opposed to men, the "healthy" woman has been viewed as submissive, less independent, less adventurous, more easily influenced, less aggressive, more excitable in minor crises, more emotional, and less objective. This double standard has placed women in an obvious conflict — ie, whether to establish behaviors considered desirable for males and thus have their femininity questioned or to behave in the prescribed feminine manner and accept "second-class status," which to many is extraordinarily demoralizing. As attitudes in this regard change concerning the healthy adult, many of the previously recognized differences between alcohol-dependent men and women may well dissolve.

Treatment Considerations

If one accepts some of the salient differences between alcohol-dependent women and men, a logical question is whether treatment approaches should also be different.[18] Until very recently, data on treatment outcome did not distinguish between men and women. In addition, success criteria for treatment outcome have been equally applied to both men and women. As a result, there is no consensus concerning the prognosis of treated alcohol-dependent women. Depending on the source, the statements have been made that the prognosis is worse than, the same as, or better than in men.

There are certain factors associated with prognosis in treated alcohol-dependent women which may differ somewhat from those in men.

Factors associated with poor prognosis include: history of familial alcoholism; serious medical complications; onset of alcohol dependence at an earlier age, ie, 20 to 30 years; concomitant use of prescribed and nonprescribed psychoactive drugs; and divorce.

Factors associated with a favorable prognosis include: association with nondrinking social groups (involvement with AA); onset of alcohol dependence at a later age, ie, 35 years or older; low SES, low educational achievement, low occupational status; higher intelligence; and concomitant affective disorder that is successfully treated.

Treatment should be directed toward improving the woman's self-image and self-esteem and resolving problems of feminine identity. It appears that women prefer and respond better to individual therapy than group counseling and psychotherapy.

The use of recovered women as therapists or cotherapists in an all-female group setting may be more beneficial than the traditional mixed-group approach. Finally, it is important for the physician to destigmatize the diagnosis of alcohol dependence in women and to refrain from the inappropriate prescription of sedative–hypnotics to these patients.

Prevention Considerations

Although considerable debate continues over the feasibility and success of various prevention techniques for alcohol dependence in general, there are two clinical practices that may be preventive with women. First, when a physician is dealing with a nonalcohol-dependent woman who is suffering a life crisis (separation, divorce, death of a spouse, etc), her increased vulnerability should be recognized. Counseling should encourage abstinence from alcohol during the crisis. In addition, the prescription of sedative–hypnotics should generally be avoided. Second, the physician should examine his or her personal attitudes toward alcohol use in women and the ways in which these attitudes affect making an earlier diagnosis of alcohol dependence in women and implementing appropriate treatment.

THE ELDERLY

Senior citizens (age 65 and older) are the second fastest growing population group in the United States today. They comprise 10% of the total population and exceed 22 million persons. It is estimated that within 20 years they will comprise 16% of the total U.S. population. Some unique characteristics of this group change the clinical complexion of alcohol dependence in the elderly.

Alcohol History

Most of the data concerning alcohol use, abuse, and dependence in the elderly derive from earlier studies that have not been replicated and from anecdotal information. It is estimated that 10% to 15% of the elderly who contact the health care delivery system for assistance have an alcohol-related problem.

Surveys indicate that the absolute number of abstainers increases and that the consumption of alcohol decreases with age. At least 5% of those persons over the age of 65 clearly suffer from alcohol dependence.

There appear to be two distinct alcohol-dependent groups in the geriatric population. One group is composed of persons whose alcohol dependence had its onset at an early age and who have "survived" to old age. Approximately two-thirds of elderly alcoholics fall into this category. A second group (one-third of the elderly alcoholics) exhibits late onset of the disease, ie, after the age of 55. The former group includes mainly the primary alcohol-dependent person; the latter group includes mainly the reactive type.[19]

Physiological Description

In regard to the CNS, many researchers have observed that neuropsychological deficits that occur as a function of the aging process are seen in alcohol-dependent patients at a younger age. This has led to the hypothesis that heavy alcohol use actually accelerates the aging process. Although the data are equivocal, it is suggested that alcohol dependence may lead to both premature aging and to organic mental disorders (brain damage) superimposed on the intrinsic aging process.[20] In clinical diagnosis, one should suspect alcohol dependence in the geriatric patient who is diagnosed as having "senile dementia." If indeed the signs and symptoms of dementia are secondary to alcohol dependence, treatment of alcoholism will frequently lead to dramatic improvement; the prognosis is much worse in persons with true senile (irreversible) dementia.

Not only do more persons become abstinent as aging progresses, but alcohol users consume less alcohol. However, one cannot assume that because less alcohol is consumed, all alcohol-related medical problems will diminish accordingly. Not only does tolerance to alcohol decrease with advancing age, but higher blood alcohol levels are achieved with standard gram per kilogram dose than would have existed at a younger age. As one grows older, the lean body mass decreases, adipose tissue increases, and the total body water decreases; therefore, there is a smaller space for the distribution of alcohol, resulting in higher blood alcohol levels. A common statement made by persons over 55 is: "I can't drink like I used to—two drinks make me tipsy."

The chronic diseases which plague the elderly are exacerbated by alcohol abuse. Although the controversy still rages concerning the alleged benefits of the "moderate use of wine" in the elderly, it is important to recognize that heart disease and diabetes mellitus, two very common maladies of the elderly, mandate against the use of any alcohol. In addition, there appears to be an association between the incidence of cancer and alcohol use in the geriatric population.

Another obvious problem is the potential for alcohol–drug interactions. Many elderly persons are taking prescribed medications for the control of various chronic illnesses. The effect of alcohol on gastrointestinal absorption and hepatic metabolism of various drugs frequently diminishes the effectiveness of the medical management of the patient.[21]

Psychological Description

Depression is observed and has been reported frequently in the elderly population. The depressive symptoms are often more of a dysthymic nature than representative of a unipolar affective illness. Among the factors that contribute to the depression are: pharmacological effects of alcohol abuse; consequences of retirement, such as boredom, loss of income, a change from a productive to an externally and internally perceived nonproductive status; existential anxiety secondary to deaths in relatives and friends; increased awareness of one's mortality; health problems associated with the aging process; loneliness; and awareness that cognitive and motor functions are deteriorating and that previously successful skills to cope with stress are effectively diminished.

All too frequently, medication is prescribed for the depression although these important factors have not been adequately addressed.[19]

Due to the effect of aging on the CNS, elderly alcohol-dependent patients are more prone to develop both classical and atypical alcoholic psychoses. Schizophrenic symptoms such as auditory/visual hallucinations and delusions, if caused by alcohol, will generally clear when the alcohol problem is treated. Many of these patients have an acute delirium characterized by disorientation for time and place, impaired consciousness, retardation, and exhaustion. In all cases, alcohol must be considered as a possible cause, since this is a form of reversible delirium with proper diagnosis and treatment.

Social Description

Just as the assumption that "most alcoholics are on skid row" is erroneous, so too is the idea that "most of the elderly live in nursing homes." Only 4% to 5% of persons over 65 reside in institutions, primarily nursing homes. Of those in nursing homes, 50% have no living relatives. Some demographic dimensions of the 95% of the elderly who live in the community are[19,20]:

1. Of elderly men, 1.6 million (17% of the total population of men over age 65) live alone or with nonrelatives.
2. Of women, 5.5 million (45% of the total population of women over age 65) live alone or with nonrelatives.
3. Of those over 65, 77% of the men, but only 48% of the women are married. Loneliness is an extremely severe stress for elderly women.
4. Currently, in the over-65 group, the average years of education is 9.5. However, there is a trend toward higher educational levels in the elderly, which will have impact on health care education and planning for this group.

From the above description, it is evident that social isolation and alienation certainly plague the elderly and are important in designing a meaningful treatment approach.

Treatment Considerations

The most important obstacle to overcome in the treatment of the elderly alcohol-dependent patient is the attitude that advanced age is incompatible with active treatment and a favorable prognosis. Because of this, identification and diagnosis of the elderly alcoholic has been approached with limited enthusiasm. New initiatives in this regard have generated information suggesting that treatment outcomes for the elderly may be more positive than for younger age groups. Furthermore, those persons suffering the onset of alcohol dependence later in life (over the age of 55) appear to respond better to treatment than do those "survivors" who have a long history of alcohol dependence.[22]

Although the elderly may not require the intensive detoxification often necessary for younger persons, the amount of time required for detoxification may be longer, and although no "special" treatment methods have been identified as universally applicable to the elderly alcohol-dependent population, there are certain guidelines that have proven helpful. First, behavior-oriented psychotherapy may be more helpful than in-depth, dynamically oriented psychotherapy. Second, it is essential to offer the full range of medical services for the treatment not only of alcohol-related complications, but of other chronic diseases as well. Third, the use of sedative–hypnotics should be minimized. In those patients who manifest significant depression, antidepressant medication (with dosage lowered because of age) combined with a range of services may be beneficial in certain cases. Fourth, addressing the need for decreasing the loneliness and social isolation is essential. Redefining a social support system, which can include volunteer activities, recreational programs, and, in some cases, vocational rehabilitation, improves the prognosis. In my experience, active affiliation with Senior Citizens is more effective than AA, unless the latter is composed primarily of elderly persons. Fifth, intensive follow-up and aftercare, even with home visitations, are important.

To care for the elderly alcohol-dependent patient appropriately, the physician must not only be willing to suspect, identify, and diagnose the problem in the 10% to 15% of the elderly who contact the health care system for medical and psychiatric problems, but also to extend case-finding to the geriatric population in general. Furthermore, the physician should vigorously oppose the culturally rooted therapeutic nihilism that results in treatment apathy and prognostic pessimism for the elderly and should be outspoken in regard to the treatment success that can be enjoyed by aggressively managing alcohol problems in this population.

Prevention Considerations

Prevention efforts need to be directed at both the 55 to 64 and over-65 age groups. Although educational efforts in the name of prevention have met with only limited success in younger age groups, it is feasible that education through the communications media might be more effective with the elderly, since their exposure to newspapers, radio, and television is often more intense than it is in younger age groups. Education should not only emphasize the medical–psychiatric risks of alcohol use, but should also deal with the anticipated loneliness, isolation, loss of income, increase in free time, inevitability of death, health problems associated with aging, and the cultural stigma of "being old" as critical issues that demand the acquisition of new coping skills.

Finally, the physician must view with great caution the statement that the "moderate use of alcoholic beverages has advantages in the elderly." This assumption is based on short-term studies, which have been unable to distinguish between the advantages of the social setting and the advantage of alcohol per se. It is perfectly legitimate for the physician to advise abstinence from alcohol for the elderly rather than prescribe "moderate" alcohol use.

PHYSICIANS

The estimate that between 10% to 12% of practicing physicians suffer a degree of impairment sufficient to compromise the quality of care delivered, thereby jeopardizing the public's welfare, is indeed frightening.

Alcohol History

Although the major problems of physicians have been identified as alcohol dependence, drug dependence, depression and suicide, and bad marriages, alcohol and/or drug dependence are the primary problems in ~ 80% of impaired physicians. Alcohol dependence is often precedent to dependence on other drugs, with an estimated 50% of all alcohol-dependent physicians being dependent on other drugs. The most common drugs of dependence are the sedative–hypnotics, stimulants, and synthetic analgesics.

According to Talbott,[23] there is a predictably sequential deterioration in a physician as measured by performance in: (a) the community; (b) family; (c) employment; (d) physical function; (e) office function; and (f) hospital function.

Community Function

Isolation and withdrawal of the physician from community activities, leisure activities and hobbies, church, friends, and peers occurs; often the physician exhibits embarrassing behavior at club or parties and incurs arrest for driving while intoxicated, in addition to other legal problems. There is unreliability and unpredictability in community and social activities, along with unpredictable behavior, eg, inappropriate spending or excessive involvement in political activities.

Family Function

The physician withdraws from family activities, with unexplained absences from home. There are fights and child abuse; development in the spouse of the disease of "spousaholism"; abnormal, antisocial, illegal behavior on the part of the children; sexual problems such as impotence, extramarital affairs and contracultural sexual behavior. There is assumption of surrogate role by the spouse and children, and often institution of geographic separation or divorce proceedings by the spouse.

Employment Stability

The alcohol-dependent physician is often characterized by numerous job changes in the past five years, frequent geographic relocations for unexplained reasons, a complicated and elaborate medical history, and unexplained intervals between jobs. Often the physician has indefinite or inappropriate references and is working in a job inappropriate for his or her qualifications. The physician may be reluctant to permit the spouse and children to be interviewed or to undergo immediate preemployment physical examination.

Physical Status

The physician allows personal hygiene and clothing and dressing habits to deteriorate and has multiple physical signs and complaints. In addition, the physician may make use of numerous prescription drugs, may have frequent hospitalizations, makes frequent visits to physicians and dentists, and experiences accidents and emotional crises.

Office Function

There may be disruption of the physician's appointment schedule and hostile, withdrawn, and unreasonable behavior to staff and patients ("locked-door syndrome"). Frequent occurrences are: excessive ordering of supplies of drugs from local druggists or by mail; complaints by patients to staff about the physician's behavior; and absence from office, either unexplained or due to frequent illness.

Hospital Function

The affected physician may make rounds late or exhibit inappropriate, abnormal behavior during rounds. There is decreasing quality of performance (eg, in staff presentations, writing in chart) and inappropriate orders or overprescription of medications. Often, there are reports of behavior changes from hospital personnel ("hospital gossip"); there may be involvement in malpractice suits together with legal sanctions against the hospital, and reports from emergency department staff of unavailability of the physician or inappropriate responses by the physician to telephone calls.

Physiological Description

Although the concomitant abuse of other drugs places the alcohol-dependent physician at higher risk for medical complications, the usual pathophysiological states affecting alcohol-dependent persons also affect physicians. In a study of 98 alcoholic physicians, Bissell[24] reported the following complications in decreasing order of frequency: gastritis, peripheral neuropathy, severe malnutrition, fatty liver, gastrointestinal bleeding, peptic ulcer, pancreatitis, cirrhosis of the liver, and esophageal varices. These conditions are characteristic of advanced and severe alcohol dependence. Physicians are more often admitted to general hospitals for these disorders, since it is easier to avoid dealing with the alcohol problem in such a setting. In addition, physicians are notorious for treating themselves and disregarding the "well-being concept" by not having a regular physician of their own and by avoiding routine, preventive examinations. These practices often permit the alcohol dependence to be more progressive, so that intervention is not afforded until the later stages of these diseases.

Psychological Description

Throughout training, the physician is taught, and indeed learns, that the ideal attributes of a successful physician are intelligence, aspiration to excellence, self-denial, and compulsivity. The physician functions in an ethical system which demands that "everything should be done for all who seek help." However, technological advances in medicine are continually defining and redefining what physicians may do and what physicians must do. Within the framework of doing all for everyone, physicians often perceive failure to fulfill personal ethical commitments and to meet society's expectations — which frequently are unreasonable and/or impossible. The physician then has two choices: (a) to accept limitations of his or her capabilities; or (b) to engage in personally destructive behaviors. Those who choose the latter generally become impaired.[25,26]

As is true in the general population, an "alcoholic personality" has not been identified as applicable to physicians. However, there are some psychological traits that emerge as thematic in physicians who manifest impairment as alcohol and/or drug dependence. Among these traits are: (a) obsessive–compulsive behaviors, often of neurotic dimensions; (b) secondary anhedonia for the sake of "doing all for everyone"; (c) self-perceived feelings of omniscience, omnipotence, and indispensability; (d) inability to tolerate failure; and (e) lack of creativity and flexibility.

Importantly, these traits are usually apparent during the medical school and postgraduate training periods.[26,27]

Studies reveal that nearly 75% of alcohol/drug-dependent physicians experience emotional impoverishment during childhood and adolescence. In addition to the usual causes of deprivation, such as divorce, death of a parent, and illness of a parent, impaired physicians often describe a distant relationship with the father and a compromised relationship with the mother, who typically is characterized as being rigid, domineering, perfectionistic, puritanical, and impersonal.[28]

Depression has been observed in over 60% of physicians presenting with alcohol/drug dependence. Little is known concerning whether the depression is a primary or a secondary process due to the pharmacological and behavioral consequences of alcohol/drug dependence. In addition, depression can be an expected sequela of the self-realization that one is not omniscient, omnipotent, and indispensable, and that failure is indigenous to the practice of medicine. The average age of onset of depression, regardless of the personality organization, is age 40 years, which is also the average age when alcohol/drug dependence appears to become clinically manifest.

Attempts have been made to differentiate alcohol/drug-dependent physicians into separate (albeit overlapping) psychodiagnostic categories. A study involving 50 addicted physicians revealed that 36% were classified in the high-level personality organization group, ie, personality disorders of the obsessive–compulsive, histrionic, or mixed varieties; 32% were classified in the intermediate-level personality organization group, ie, personality disorders of the narcissistic, avoidant, or schizoid varieties; 28% were classified as having a borderline personality organization; and 4% were suffering psychotic states, ie, schizophrenia, manic psychosis.

As mentioned previously, depression as a clinical syndrome occurs in 60% to 65% of alcohol/drug-dependent physicians regardless of the personality pathology. If the onset of alcohol/drug dependence occurs before age 40 years, more serious psychopathology, usually of the borderline type, appears to be predominant. If the onset occurs past age 40 years, organic mental disorders and depression appear to be predominant.

As with any patient, a differential diagnosis of associated psychopathology is essential to treatment approaches and pertinent to treatment outcome expectations. It can no longer be assumed that graduation from medical school is tantamount to "good mental health," and that physicians subsequently become impaired solely as a reaction to the stress of medical practice.

Social Description

The few studies that have attempted to ascertain the incidence of alcohol/drug dependence according to medical specialty are plagued by relatively small sample numbers; nevertheless, there appears to be a general trend. Those specialties in which the incidence of alcohol/drug-dependent physicians is proportionately greater than what one would expect in regard to the representative percentage of physicians in that specialty include family practice, obstetrics and gynecology, psychiatry, and anesthesiology. However, impairment secondary to alcohol and/or drugs is found in all medical specialties.

The first areas in the social system to suffer as a result of alcohol/drug dependence in the physician are the functioning of the nuclear family and involvement in community activities. Deterioration in these areas frequently precedes deterioration in clinical performance. Examination of the medical marriage reveals that 47% of physicians (not all of whom are alcohol/drug dependent) report "bad marriages," and 75% of physicians who are dependent on alcohol and/or drugs report sexual difficulties within the marriage. To complicate matters, a significant number of physicians' wives suffer psychiatric and alcohol/drug-dependence problems, with the onset at approximately the same age as the husband, ie, age 40 years. If the impaired physician turns to the wife for help, her depression and/or alcohol–drug problem obviate effective intervention, and the family constellation progresses to the midrange and severely dysfunctional stages.[25]

Other social behaviors of the impaired physician which can be consequent to the impairment process include extramarital affairs, excessive spending on material things, overinvolvement in high-risk investments, inappropriate business ventures, and gambling.

It has also been found that many physicians who become impaired are from lower income families and have difficulty handling their economic success as physicians. Other forms of social disruption are outlined previously under "Alcohol History."

All physicians are challenged with dealing with a multiple family system — the nuclear and extended families, the community family, the hospital family, and the office family. Physicians in the best of health find this responsibility rewarding, albeit challenging and often difficult. Dysfunction in coping with these families is often an early sign of impairment and only escalates as the impairment progresses in severity.

Treatment Considerations

The adage that the "most difficult and challenging patient to treat is another physician" certainly applies to the management of the impaired physician. There are a number of factors that must be considered.

Generally, there are more medical–psychiatric complications in the physician–patient because he or she has resisted intervention until the impairment has become overtly obvious to everyone.

Even with impairment, the physician frequently has not relinquished the self-imposed and societally imposed omniscience and omnipotence; thus, accepting the patient role is extremely difficult.

Hostility, denial, and manipulation of the therapist and treatment staff often results in minimizing the severity of the condition and/or underdiagnosing the problem.

Recognizing that most physicians who enter treatment are coerced with the threat of licensure suspension or revocation can assist the treatment team in dissolving the consummate denial so characteristic of the physician–patient.

The suicide potential of the impaired physician is very high, particularly after confrontation and in the early phases of treatment. After the physician is confronted with his or her impairment, it is critical to access the evaluation and treatment processes immediately. Any delay significantly increases the suicide risk. In most cases, inpatient treatment is initially necessary. There is still controversy over whether the impaired physician should be treated in a program with other physicians (and health professionals) or in a setting with nonphysicians. Although each case should be considered individually, I and others, feel that treatment in a facility that has expertise in the management of chemical dependency that specializes in the care of physicians and other health professionals is preferable. Experience in dealing with the denial, hostility, and manipulation, in addition to the value of common professional identities, are essential ingredients for a consistently positive treatment outcome. Self-help groups such as AA and NA, on both an inpatient and outpatient basis, are extremely valuable and usually more effective if composed primarily of physicians.

The success of treatment is directly related to the skill and speed used in the detection and reporting of the impaired physician, the confrontation (early intervention) and the evaluation—all processes which usually precede treatment. Generally, the inpatient experience should take place outside of the community of the impaired physician; however, the geographical distance should not obviate involving the family and significant others (ie, colleagues) in the treatment program.

Outpatient treatment is essential and can consist of one or a combination of AA (International Doctors of AA), Cadeuceus clubs, NA, and individual psychotherapy. Treatment should be clearly differentiated from monitoring, which consists of insuring compliance with treatment recommendations— urine–drug screens, Antabuse therapy, review of records to assess conformity with established standards of care, etc. The person(s) conducting treatment should be other than those responsible for the monitoring process.

Initially, there was a prognostic pessimism about the recovery of the impaired physician, in view of the hostility, denial, manipulation, and advanced stages of impairment encountered; however, the few outcome studies that have been published report a range of 60% to 85% recovery, defined as "serene sobriety" and effective reentry into the community, family, and practice of medicine.[23,29] The impaired physician is treatable, and recovery is certainly a realistic expectation.

Prevention Considerations

Early efforts by impaired physicians programs were designed to address tertiary prevention. Quite naturally, as experience was acquired in the identification and reporting, confrontation (early intervention), evaluation, treatment, and monitoring of impaired physicians, it became obvious that physicians are not omniscient and omnipotent and are certainly vulnerable to alcohol and/or drug dependence and psychological problems (especially depression), perhaps to a greater degree than the nonphysician population. As knowledge increased about the profile of the impaired physician, attention was directed at secondary prevention (early case finding) and primary prevention. In regard to the latter, it has been suggested that there be an increase in integrated didactic and experiential training for both medical students and postgraduate physicians in the area of alcohol and drug dependence. Establishment of programs for the impaired medical student have been recommended. It is estimated that for all identified impaired physicians, in 25% to 30% of the cases some degree of impairment was manifest during the medical school training period. Such programs are also recommended for the impaired resident. It is also important that prevention programs be developed for high-risk groups within the physician population, such as aging physicians and women physicians.

Medical schools, medical societies, and medical auxiliaries should place more emphasis on physician health ("well-being") and on the well-being of the family system. Such emphasis should embrace the fundamentals of well-being articulated by Menninger: (a) ability to function under difficulty; (b) capacity to change; (c) freedom from symptoms of anxiety and tension; (d) ability to give rather than to receive; (e) ability to get along with others; and (f) ability to deal with anger while recognizing the need to love.

The differentiation between what physicians "must do" and what physicians "can do" is one of the foundations of any well-being philosophy. The public good mandates that the physician community, on both an individual and collective basis, identify and treat physician illness behaviors and vigorously promote healthy behaviors.

REFERENCES

1. Hanson JW: The effect of moderate alcohol consumption during pregnancy on fetal growth and morphogenesis. *J Pediatr* 92:457–560, 1978.
2. Jones KL, Smith DW: Recognition of the fetal alcohol syndrome in early infancy. *Lancet* 2:999–1001, 1973.
3. Ouellette EM: Adverse effects on offspring of maternal alcohol abuse during pregnancy. *N Engl J Med* 298:1063–1067, 1977.
4. Streissguth AP, Landesman-Dwyer S, Martin JC, Smith DW: Teratogenic effects of alcohol in humans and laboratory animals. *Science* 209:353–361, 1980.
5. Streissguth AP: A fetal alcohol syndrome: An epidemiological perspective. *Am J Epidemiol* 107:467–478, 1978.
6. Clarren SK, Smith DW: The fetal alcohol syndrome. *N Engl J Med* 298:1063–1067, 1978.
7. Fetal effects of maternal alcohol use. AMA Report of the Council on Scientific Affairs. 1982: Report E (A-82).
8. Abel EL: Fetal alcohol syndrome: Behavioral teratology. *Psychol Bull* 87(1):29–50, 1980.
9. Filstead WJ: Adolescence and alcohol, in Pattison EM, Kaufman E (eds): *Encyclopedic Handbook of Alcoholism*. New York, Gardner, 1982, pp 769–778.
10. Pandina RJ, White HR: Patterns of alcohol and drug use of adolescent students and adolescents in treatment. *J Stud Alcohol* 39(9):1506–1524, 1978.
11. Donovan JE, Jessor R: Adolescent problem drinking. *J Stud Alcohol* 39(9):1506–1524, 1978.
12. Gharderian AM: Adolescent alcoholism: Motives and alternatives. *Compr Psychiatry* 29(5):469–474, 1979.
13. Lisansky ES: Alcoholism and women: Social and psychological concomitants. *Q J Stud Alcohol* 18:588–623, 1957.
14. Wilsnack CS: Alcohol abuse and alcoholism in women, in Pattison EM, Kaufman E (eds): *Encyclopedic Handbook of Alcoholism*. New York, Gardner, 1982, pp 718–735.

15. Glatt MM: Reflections on the treatment of alcoholism in women. *Br J Alcohol and Alcoholism* 14(2):77-83, 1979.
16. Greenblatt M, Schuckit MA (eds): *Alcoholism Problems in Women and Children.* Orlando, Fla, Grune & Stratton, 1976.
17. Hill SY: A vulnerability model for alcoholism in women. *J Addict and Health* 2(2):68-91, 1982.
18. Hennecke L, Fox V: The woman with alcoholism, in Gitlow SE, Peyser HS (eds): *Alcoholism: A Practical Treatment Guide,* Orlando, Fla, Grune & Stratton, 1980, pp 181-192.
19. Brody JA: Aging and alcohol abuse. *Grassroots* 1982:11-14.
20. Maletta GJ: Alcoholism and the aged, in Pattison EM, Kaufman E (eds): *Encyclopedic Handbook of Alcoholism,* New York, Gardner, 1982, pp 779-801.
21. Vestal RE, McGuire EA, Tobin JD, Andres R, Norris AH, Mezey E: Aging and ethanol metabolism. Clin Parmacol Ther 21(3):343-354, 1977.
22. Mishara BL, Kastenbaum R: Alcohol and old age, in Greenblatt M (ed): *Seminars in Psychiatry.* Orlando, Fla, Grune & Stratton, 1980, pp 1-215.
23. Talbott GD, Beson EB: Impaired physicians — The dilemma of identification. *Postgrad Med* 66(6):56-64, 1980.
24. Bissell L, Jones RW: The alcoholic physician — A survey. *Am J Psychiatry* 133(10):1142-1146, 1976.
25. Schieber SC: Emotional problems of physicians — Nature and extent of problems. Ariz Med 34(5):323-325, 1977.
26. Robertson JJ (ed): The impaired physician, Proceedings of the Third AMA Conference on the Impaired Physician. Department of Mental Health, American Medical Association 1978:1-96.
27. Robertson JJ (ed): The impaired physician — building well-being, Proceedings of the Fourth AMA Conference on the Impaired Physician. Department of Mental Health, American Medical Association 1980:1-173.
28. Johnson RP, Connelly JC: Addicted physicians — A closer look. *JAMA* 245(3):253-257, 1981.
29. Shore JH: The impaired physician — Four years after probation. *JAMA* 248(23):3127-3130, 1982.

Chapter 9
THE ALCOHOLISMS:
RESEARCH PERSPECTIVES ON
CONTROL AND PREVENTION

In every society the classification of disease — the nosology — mirrors social organization. The sickness that society produces is baptized by the doctor with names that bureaucrats cherish.[1]

Although major advances appear to have been made during the past two decades concerning the knowledge of the "nature and nurture" of alcoholism, the approach to control and prevention is sharply divided. There are those policy-makers who believe that control of the offending agent (alcohol) would minimize the seriousness of alcohol abuse/dependence. On the other hand, those who support the premise that only a fraction of persons who use alcohol develop alcohol abuse/dependence assert that control measures should be directed toward this fraction (the host). Thus, the "baptizing and cherishing" of this sickness is confounded by the *agent v host* controversy, a public health dilemma.

A communicable disease model of the alcoholisms, which includes agent–host–vector, lends a perspective to this area that encourages, even demands, cooperative efforts. A classical example of a communicable disease is viral encephalitis in which the agent is the virus, the host is a human (especially the central nervous system in humans), and the vector is a mosquito. With the alcoholisms, the paradigm is: agent, alcohol; host, human (with emphasis on high-risk groups); and vector, the distributing system, ie, the sociocultural milieu. If research in regard to control and prevention efforts does not embrace all three components of this model, divisiveness and regressive tactics shall surely prevail.[2]

The following discussion, albeit limited, attempts to highlight some research concepts and opportunities in regard to the agent–host–vector model.

AGENT

Whenever medicine has been faced with an apparently effective but toxic drug, research has attempted to diminish the toxicity while preserving the effectiveness of the drug. Although one may argue the question of the "efficacy" of alcohol, its wide use by millions of Americans who can drink without problems is testimony to society's perception of effectiveness. Little attention has been focused on reducing the toxicity of beverage alcohol other than reducing the concentration of ethanol.

Many contend that the congeners found in beverage alcohol are in themselves harmful and, in addition, may augment the toxicity of ethyl alcohol. Reduction and/or neutralization of the toxicity of congeners (ie, methyl alcohol, higher alcohols, aldehydes, esters, tannins, etc) may attenuate the adverse physiological and biochemical effects of beverage alcohol.

I had a brief research experience with a southern distillery that was attempting to change the physical properties of its brand of vodka. In essence, the concentration of various salts was changed to make the beverage isotonic with body fluids. A review of the plethora of anecdotal information (primarily letters from physicians) suggested the absence of a "hangover" after consumption of large quantities of this isotonic vodka. Research focused on studying absorption rates, metabolic rates, acetaldehyde levels, etc. Data revealed no difference between this isotonic vodka and a commercially available, nonisotonic vodka. Unfortunately, the distillery was not interested in pursuing further research in this regard. However, the concept is intriguing: Perhaps changing the physical properties and chemical (congeners) composition could preserve the "psychological blessings" and diminish the "physiological curse" of beverage alcohol.

There is still some interest in adding various vitamins, minerals, and nutrients to alcohol, all of which might decrease toxicity. These efforts have met with only limited success because certain additives alter the taste of the beverage, which in turn has impact on consumer acceptance. In addition, certain advertising techniques which have implied that nutritionally fortified alcoholic beverages are "healthy" have incurred the wrath of those who believe that the alcoholisms are solely due to the agent alcohol.

Although significant political ambivalence toward and, at times, overt obstruction of basic research efforts plague the alcoholism field, it is imperative that such studies continue and be renewed.[3] Of particular interest would be studies designed to:

1. Determine genetic differences among humans in alcohol dehydrogenases.
2. Identify and evaluate the mode of action of the isoenzymes of human alcohol dehydrogenase.
3. Explore further the contribution of alternate metabolic pathways of alcohol, such as the microsomal ethanol oxidizing system and the catalase-

dependent oxidation system. What influence do these systems have on the toxicity of ethanol? Can these systems be manipulated to reduce toxicity?

4. Develop animal models further; the response of animals to alcohol simulates that of humans. The development and biochemical evaluation of genetic strains of animals associated with different responses to alcohol could be of particular value.
5. Investigate further the mechanisms of tolerance, particularly the effect of alcohol on Ca^{2+} ion distribution in membranes of the central nervous system (CNS) and the relationship of this effect to the development of tolerance to other drugs, particularly the opiates.
6. Define further the influence exerted by the lipid composition of cell membranes on cellular and organ system response to alcohol.
7. Intensify investigative efforts in regard to the effects of alcohol on neurotransmitter function, ie, the concentration, turnover, localization, and action of transmitters, the effect of alcohol on alteration of the structure and metabolism of neurotransmitters; and the acute and chronic effects of alcohol on benzodiazepine receptors, particularly in regard to the action of gamma aminobutyric acid.

The above are only a few examples of potentially fruitful areas of basic research. It is imperative that the alcohol research enterprise continue with basic research efforts and vigorously oppose those who would channel the bulk of research monies solely into the treatment system.

HOST

In regard to that fraction of the drinking population which develops alcohol abuse/dependence, there is increasing interest in genetic influences and also in inherited and acquired individual differences in susceptibility to the effects of alcohol.

Prior to the 1970s, there was considerable ambivalence concerning the usefulness of genetic research in alcoholism. The increased incidence of alcoholism in families was attributed primarily to environmental factors. However, a few investigators pursued "inheritance factors" for alcoholism; currently, there is substantial evidence that genetic influences are operational in the etiology of alcoholism in some persons. In brief, studies have shown the following: (a) in twin studies, in which one twin was an alcohol abuser, in 70% of monozygotic twins, but in only 32% of dizygotic twins, the other twin was also; (b) sons of alcoholic parent(s) separated from parents early in life were four times more likely to become alcoholics than were adoptees without alcoholic biological parents; and (c) there does not appear to be a well-defined genetic contribution to the development of alcoholism in adopted and nonadopted daughters of an alcoholic parent(s). However, there is some indication that there is a higher incidence of depression in these adopted or non-adopted daughters.

Although the environmentally oriented antagonists of the inherited disease concept of alcoholism can point out methodological problems in the genetic studies reported thus far, it appears likely that genetic factors do contribute to alcoholism in men, and possibly in women.

The question of what is inherited still remains. Is it a biochemical predisposition for alcoholism, perhaps involving genetically linked differences in alcohol dehydrogenase and/or aldehyde dehydrogenase so that the metabolism of alcohol is changed in such a way as to cause biologically the "loss of control" phenomenon? Basic research has shown that inbred strains of rats and mice that exhibit a preference for the voluntary consumption of alcohol have a higher alcohol dehydrogenase activity. The search for genetic markers in humans has revealed an association between alcoholism and (a) the non-secretion of ABH blood group substances in saliva, and (b) below-normal platelet MAO activity. These findings imply that it may be possible to use a biological marker to detect genetically determined, high-risk individuals before the onset of alcohol abuse/dependence.

The question of what is different about the fraction of alcohol users who develop alcohol abuse/dependence still remains. The genetic explanation accounts for only certain cases. Are there other psychological and sociocultural differences which predispose a person to the alcoholisms that are not influenced by heredity and that are not the consequences of heavy drinking? Most research to date has focused on studying "alcoholic" patients, and the differences in these areas that have been found are usually attributed to the consequences of excessive alcohol use. They are usually not considered to be differences that existed a priori that may have increased susceptibility.

In regard to psychological factors, an interesting area for future study is research on the cognitive development of adolescents. There is evidence to suggest that adolescents do not have the ability to make valid generalizations, to use symbols, and to process information with objectivity. Does this increase susceptibility to the effects of alcohol? Does alcohol impair cognitive maturation and, if so, is this a factor in the later development of alcohol abuse/dependence? Does regression from mature, abstract levels of cognitive functioning precede the development of alcohol abuse/dependence or occur as a result? As implied previously, carefully planned, longitudinal research on drinking and nondrinking adolescents, particularly concerning the association between alcohol use, cognitive maturation, and physical maturation, should yield valuable information about critical psychological factors in the development of alcohol abuse/dependence in adults.

Although no "alcoholic personality" has yet been clearly defined, further research is needed concerning the major psychiatric disorders that are associated with alcohol abuse/dependence. An exciting area in this regard is the association between depression and alcohol abuse/dependence. Clinical depression associated with heavy drinking must be more clearly defined as being either etiological for, or consequential to, alcohol abuse/dependence. There is some speculation that alcoholism and depression may share a common genetic link and that alcoholism may be part of a "depressive disease spectrum" in some patients.

In regard to sociocultural factors which affect the susceptibility of the host, it is agreed that alcohol consumption patterns, alcohol-related behaviors, and alcohol-related problems vary among cultural groups and levels of society, and that issues such as family dynamics, parenting behaviors, and the level and degree of socialization significantly alter host susceptibility.

Research has revealed that the following sociocultural conditions are associated with less excessive drinking and fewer alcohol-related problems.[4]

1. The children are exposed to alcohol early in life within a strong family or religious group. Whatever the beverage, it is served in very diluted form and in small quantities, with consequent low blood-alcohol levels.

2. The beverages commonly although not invariably used by the groups are those containing relatively large amounts of non-alcoholic components, which also give low blood-alcohol levels.

3. The beverage is considered mainly as a food and usually consumed with meals, again with consequent low blood-alcohol levels.

4. Parents present a constant example of moderate drinking.

5. No moral importance is attached to drinking. It is considered neither a virtue nor a sin.

6. Drinking is not viewed as a proof of adulthood or virility.

7. Abstinence is socially acceptable. It is no more rude or ungracious to decline a drink than to decline a piece of bread.

8. Excessive drinking or intoxication is not socially acceptable. It is not considered stylish, comical, or tolerable.

9. . . . there is wide and usually complete agreement among members of the group on what might be called the ground rules of drinking.

Future investigation should not only continue to validate these conditions, but should also search for additional sociocultural variables associated with both high-risk and low-risk populations. The education and prevention implications of such conditions are obvious.

VECTOR

Alcohol has been called the "cultural tranquilizer" for the United States. The active condoning and encouraging of alcohol use in our society and, at the same time, the stigmatizing of those persons who develop alcohol abuse/dependence is a significant perplexity which generates ambivalence toward and obstruction of advancement in this field. The evaluation of attempts to control the distribution (vector) of the alcohol agent in society is seriously compromised by this societal ambivalence.

Attempts that have been implemented to control the distribution of alcohol include: restriction of the availability of alcohol by changing zoning laws, and effecting minimum age requirements and rules governing the number of, hours of, and location of outlets for the purchase of alcohol; and decrease in the daily consumption index by raising prices and increasing taxation.

To date, there is no clear evidence that these measures reduce alcohol-related problems. However, further research is needed in this area. There appears to be some validity to the concept that an increase in per capita consumption is associated with an increase in heavy alcohol use, which in turn is associated with an increase in medical, social, and psychological problems caused by alcohol. After reviewing the past and current effects of restraint measures, three conclusions appear evident[4]: (a) highly restrictive controls do lead to lower consumption and fewer alcohol problems; (b) highly restrictive controls are not likely to be successfully implemented unless there is substantial public support; and (c) such controls involve social and political manipulations which, over a period of time, may not be cost-effective.

Thus far, the political and financial power of the alcohol beverage industry plus the societal ambivalence toward drinking *v* alcohol abuse/dependence has rendered restrictive measures for the most part ineffective as a prevention and control technique.

In addition to assessing the impact of control measures as outlined above, social research should address those procedures that allegedly influence beliefs, attitudes, and behavioral choices. What is the relationship between the pervasive portrayal of drinking situations in the communications media and the incidence of alcohol use and alcohol-related problems in various populations? Although much rhetoric asserts that such media messages exert a significant influence on drinking patterns, no replicated studies to date have unequivocally validated such an assertion.

What is the effect of alcohol education of children, adolescents, and adults on the incidence of alcohol use and alcohol-related problems? Statements that educational efforts are preventive in nature cannot be substantiated, since there has been no critical evaluation in this area.

Finally, if science and craft can effectively join in a research effort, the issue of treatment effectiveness and outcome can be critically evaluated. In this regard, attention must be directed toward "spontaneous" remissions, toward persons who seek but never find treatment, toward the characteristics of those persons who utilize treatment services and the manner in which those services are utilized, toward persons who recover through treatment, toward persons who do not recover through treatment, and toward persons who may be at high risk—ie, the host whose individual susceptibility may be altered by genetic and/or psychological and/or sociocultural factors.

Although research involving the agent–host–vector system may shift in priorities and may sporadically result in clinically applicable advances, I do not anticipate any major breakthroughs in the diagnosis, treatment, and prevention of alcohol abuse/dependence until there is a significant change in this society's attitude toward the individual and collective responsibility of understanding and coping with the fundamental, human existential dilemma. Currently, humans embrace the concept of "better living through chemistry." Thus, the American public, through self-medication (alcohol) and/or prescribed medication (tranquilizers), attempts to obliterate the normative anxiety and depression consequent to "adapting to changing environments, to growing up, to aging, to suffering, to healing when damaged, and to the expectation of death."[1] When humans can appreciate that health is an "adaptation to consciously lived fragility, individuality and relatedness," the ambience in which research designed to understand better not only the disease spectrum of the alcoholisms but chronic diseases in general would evolve and could contribute consummately to the quality of human life.

Such an ambience is the fantasy of many. But, in the meantime, if the practicing physician in dealing with the diseases of alcoholism will follow the adage that: "He who is sick should find in the eyes of the physician, a reflection of his own anguish and some recognition of the uniqueness of his suffering,"[1] that physician will have positive impact on this nation's number one public health problem.

Conventional approaches based on traditional concepts have been disappointing in the control and prevention of the alcoholisms. Nonconventional approaches based on new concepts founded in further investigation of the agent–host–vector model of the alcoholisms should significantly relieve the enormous suffering caused by the alcoholisms in our society.

REFERENCES

1. Illich I: *Medical Nemesis: The Expropriation of Health*. New York, Random House, 1976.
2. Lieber CS: A public health approach for the control of the disease of alcoholism. *Alcoholism, Clin Exp Res* 2:171–177, 1982.
3. *Alcoholism, Alcohol Abuse, and Related Problems: Opportunities for Research.* Institute of Medicine, Division of Health Promotion and Disease Prevention, Washington, D.C., National Academy, 1980.
4. *Alcohol and Health.* Fourth Special Report to the US Congress, US Department of Health and Human Services, January, 1981.

Appendix A
ABSTINENCE SYMPTOM EVALUATION
(ASE) SCALE

*1. Tremor

   0 — No tremor with arms and fingers extended
   1 — Tremor of hands and fingers with arms and fingers extended
   2 — Tremor of entire upper extremity (fingers, hands, and arms)
       with arms and fingers extended
   3 — Tremor of fingers, hands and arms noticeable with no
       extension of arms and fingers

*2. Paroxysmal Sweats (within 48 hours prior to admission)

   0 — Sweating absent
   1 — Perceptible sweating nocturnally
   2 — Perceptible sweating during the day
   3 — Constant sweating, beads of sweat observable

*3. Sleep Disturbance (within 48 hours prior to admission)

   0 — Slept the entire nght
   1 — Awoke during the night but able to return to sleep
   2 — Awoke during the night but unable to return to sleep
   3 — Unable to sleep at all

*4. Anxiety (fearful, apprehensive, tense)

   0 — Absent
   1 — Mildly anxious
   2 — Moderately anxious
   3 — Acute panic state

*5. Agitation

   0 — Absent
   1 — Mild increase in motor activity

2 — Fidgety, restless — moderate increase in motor activity
3 — Unable to be still — pacing, thrashing — constant motor activity

*6. Reflexes

0 — Normoreflexic
1 — Areflexic
2 — Hyperreflexic in biceps or quadriceps
3 — Hyperreflexic in both biceps and quadriceps

*7. Temperature

0 — Normal T° 98.6
1 — Up to 99.6
2 — 99.6 to 100.6
3 — 100.6 +

*8. Blood Pressure

Age ≤ 30	Age 30-50	Age ≥ 50
0 — 120/80	0 — 130/85	0 — 140/90
1 — 130/85	1 — 140/90	1 — 150/100
2 — 140/90	2 — 150/100	2 — 160/110
3 — 150/100	3 — 160/110	3 — 170/120

*9. Pulse Rate

0 — 60 to 80
1 — 80 to 100
2 — 100 to 120
3 — > 120

*10. Seizure Activity (grand mal)

0 — No history of and absence of convulsions
1 — History of alcohol withdrawal seizures
2 — History of epilepsy not alcohol-related (may or may not have
  had alcohol withdrawal seizure)
3 — Current seizure activity (within past 24 hours)

11. Pulse Regularity

0 — Regular
1 — 1 to 3 irregular beats/minute
2 — 4 to 8 irregular beats/minute
3 — > 8 irregular beats/minute

12. Nystagmus
    0 — Absent
    1 — Horizontal nystagmus endpoint, brief
    2 — Horizontal nystagmus endpoint, sustained
    3 — Horizontal nystagmus without stimulation

13. Disturbance of Gait

    0 — Absent
    1 — Mild, unsteady, can ambulate without assistance
    2 — Moderate, unsteady, must hold onto something or have
      assistance in ambulating
    3 — Unsteady, unable to ambulate

14. Eating Disturbances (within 48 hours prior to admission)

    0 — Ate and enjoyed all of food
    1 — Ate about half of food served
    2 — Ate less than half of food served
    3 — Ate none of the food served

15. Nausea and Vomiting (within 48 hours prior to admission)

    0 — No nausea and vomiting
    1 — Nausea but no vomiting
    2 — Intermittent nausea and vomiting
    3 — Constant nausea and vomiting

16. Pruritis (within 48 hours prior to admission)

    0 — Absence of itching
    1 — Occasional mild itching
    2 — Periodic severe itching
    3 — Constant state of severe itching

17. Muscle Pain (within 48 hours prior to admission)

    0 — Absence of pain
    1 — Infrequent mild muscle pain
    2 — Periodic severe muscle pain with cramping
    3 — Constant severe muscle pain with cramping

18. Nightmares (within 48 hours prior to admission)

    0 — No unpleasant dreams
    1 — Unpleasant dreams that do not awaken patient

2—Unpleasant dreams that awaken patient, but able to return
   to sleep
3—Unable to sleep at all

19. Tinnitus (within 48 hours prior to admission)

   0—Absence of tinnitus
   1—Infrequent, transient, low intensity
   2—Moderately frequent and/or moderately loud
      and/or moderate duration
   3—Constant and loud

20. Visual Disturbances (especially blurring) (within 48 hours prior
    to admission)

   0—Absent
   1—Occurs infrequently
   2—Occurs frequently
   3—Is constant

21. Insight

   0—Understands relationship between physical symptoms
      and drinking pattern
   1—Does not understand relationship between physical
      symptoms and drinking pattern
   2—Denies any problem other than alcohol
   3—Denies any problem with alcohol

22. Quality of Contact
   0—Aware of the examiner and the environment
   1—In contact with examiner but oblivious to surroundings
      and other people
   2—Periodically is detached from examiner
   3—No contact with the examiner

23. Depression (within 48 hours prior to admission)

   0—Absent
   1—"Feeling blue," affect depressed
   2—Moderately depressed/affect depressed/psychomotor
      retardation/agitated)
   3—Severely depressed, suicidal

24. Level of Consciousness

0 — Fully alert
1 — Mildly drowsy, does not fall asleep
2 — Very drowsy, intermittently falls asleep but awakens easily
3 — Falls asleep, awakened with difficulty

25. Paresthesias (within 48 hours prior to admission)

0 — Absent
1 — Pins and needles sensation upper or lower extremities
2 — Pins and needles sensation upper and lower extremities
3 — Pins and needles sensation, burning and pain, upper and/or lower extremities

**26. Sensorium

0 — Oriented in all spheres
1 — Disoriented, time
2 — Disoriented, time, place
3 — Disoriented, time, place, person

**27. Auditory Hallucinations (within 48 hours prior to admission)

0 — Absent
1 — Transient, observing ego intact (knows that hallucinations are not real)
2 — Frequent/continuous, observing ego intact
3 — Transient/frequent/continuous, observing ego not intact

**28. Visual Hallucinations (within 48 hours prior to admission)

0 — Absent
1 — Transient, observing ego intact (knows that hallucinations are not real)
2 — Frequent/continuous, observing ego intact
3 — Transient/frequent/continuous, observing ego not intact

**29. Tactile Hallucinations (within 48 hours prior to admission)

0 — Absent
1 — Mild, occasional, observing ego intact (knows that hallucinations are not real)
2 — Moderately intense, frequent, observing ego intact
3 — Transient, moderately intense, frequent, observing ego not intact

**30. Delusions (within 48 hours prior to admission)

    0 — Absent
    1 — Present, intermittent, observing ego intact (knows
        delusions are not real)
    2 — Present, intermittent, observing ego not intact
    3 — Present and continuous, observing ego not intact

Total Score _____

 *Selected Severity Score _____
**Psychotic Score   _____

INDEX

ABOUT THE AUTHOR

Dr David Knott is Clinical Director at Memphis Mental Health Institute, Clinical Professor in Psychiatry, and Clinical Assistant Professor in Family Medicine at the University of Tennessee Center for the Health Sciences in Memphis. He received his MD (1963) and PhD in Physiology (1965) from the University of Tennessee Center for the Health Sciences. Dr Knott was a John and Mary Markle Foundation Scholar in Academic Medicine (1966–1971). Dr Knott is a former member of the Advisory Board and the Alcohol Research Review Committee of the National Institute on Alcohol Abuse and Alcoholism. Dr Knott has served on the Executive Board of the American Medical Society on Alcoholism and on the Panel of Alcoholism of the American Medical Association. Dr Knott is a faculty member of the University of Utah School on Alcoholism and Other Drug Dependencies. He is a Fellow of the American Academy of Family Physicians and a Diplomate of the American Board of Family Practice. Dr Knott and his colleague, Dr James Beard, are the recipients of the James H. Tharp Alcohol Research Award.